BEYOND PEGGY'S COVE

51 UNUSUAL AND REMARKABLE SITES IN NOVA SCOTIA

Library and Archives Canada Cataloguing in Publication

Title: Beyond Peggy's Cove : 51 unusual and remarkable sites
in Nova Scotia / Stacy Ann Milford.
Names: Milford, Stacy Ann, author.
Description: Includes bibliographical references and index.
Identifiers: Canadiana 20260126683 | ISBN 9781998220403 (softcover)
Subjects: LCSH: Nova Scotia—Guidebooks. | LCGFT: Guidebooks.
Classification: LCC FC2307 .M53 2026 | DDC 917.1604/5—dc23

Published by Boulder Books
Portugal Cove-St. Philip's, Newfoundland and Labrador
www.boulderbooks.ca

Design and layout: Tanya Montini
Editor: Stephanie Porter
Copy editor: Iona Bulgin

Printed in China

We acknowledge the financial support of the Government of Newfoundland and Labrador through the Department of Tourism, Culture, Arts and Recreation.

Funded by the Government of Canada | Financé par le gouvernement du Canada | Canada

BEYOND PEGGY'S COVE

51 UNUSUAL AND REMARKABLE SITES IN NOVA SCOTIA

BOULDER
BOOKS

STACY ANN MILFORD

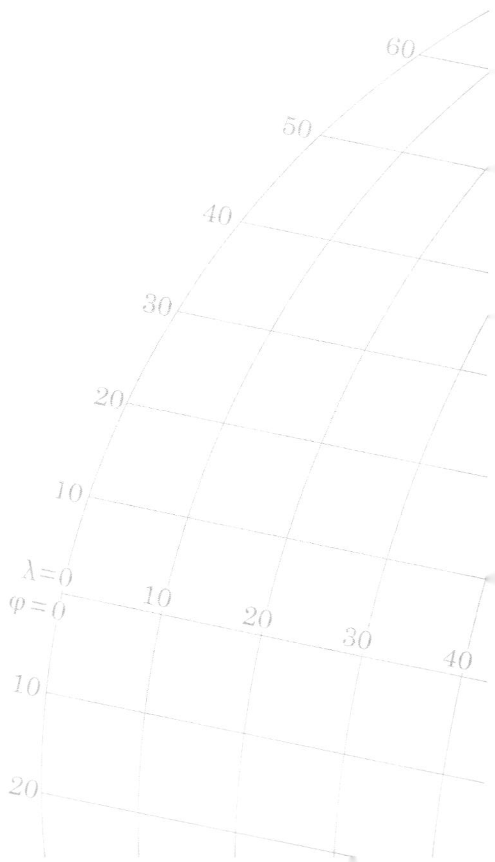
60
50
40
30
20
10
λ=0
φ=0
10
20
30
40
10
20

IN MEMORY OF
DAN MILFORD AND JIM DICK,
WHO WILL FOREVER BE
THE INSPIRATION
BEHIND MY ADVENTURES.

TABLE OF CONTENTS

47
ENTER THE BUNKER
This way!
STOP
NOTICE
THESE DOORS
MUST BE
KEPT CLOSED
NO
TRESPASSING
USE CAUTION
ON WALKWAYS

LØCATOR MAP

BAY OF FUNDY & ANNAPOLIS VALLEY

23. Acadian Dykes
24. Bear River (L'sitkuk)
25. Berlin Wall Panels
26. Blue Beach
27. Buried Ships of Summerville
28. Burntcoat Head Park
29. Courthouse Hill
30. Debert Diefenbunker
31. Balancing Rock
32. Millbrook Cultural and Heritage Centre
33. Maud Lewis Memorial Park
34. Medford Beach Sandstone Stacks
35. Concrete House and Fairy Cottages
36. The "Old Barn" on Stannus Street
37. Sinclair House
38. Stewiacke's Halfway Marker

YARMOUTH & ACADIAN SHORES

20. Argyle Township Court House and Gaol
21. Sandford Drawbridge
22. Yarmouth Buoy Wall

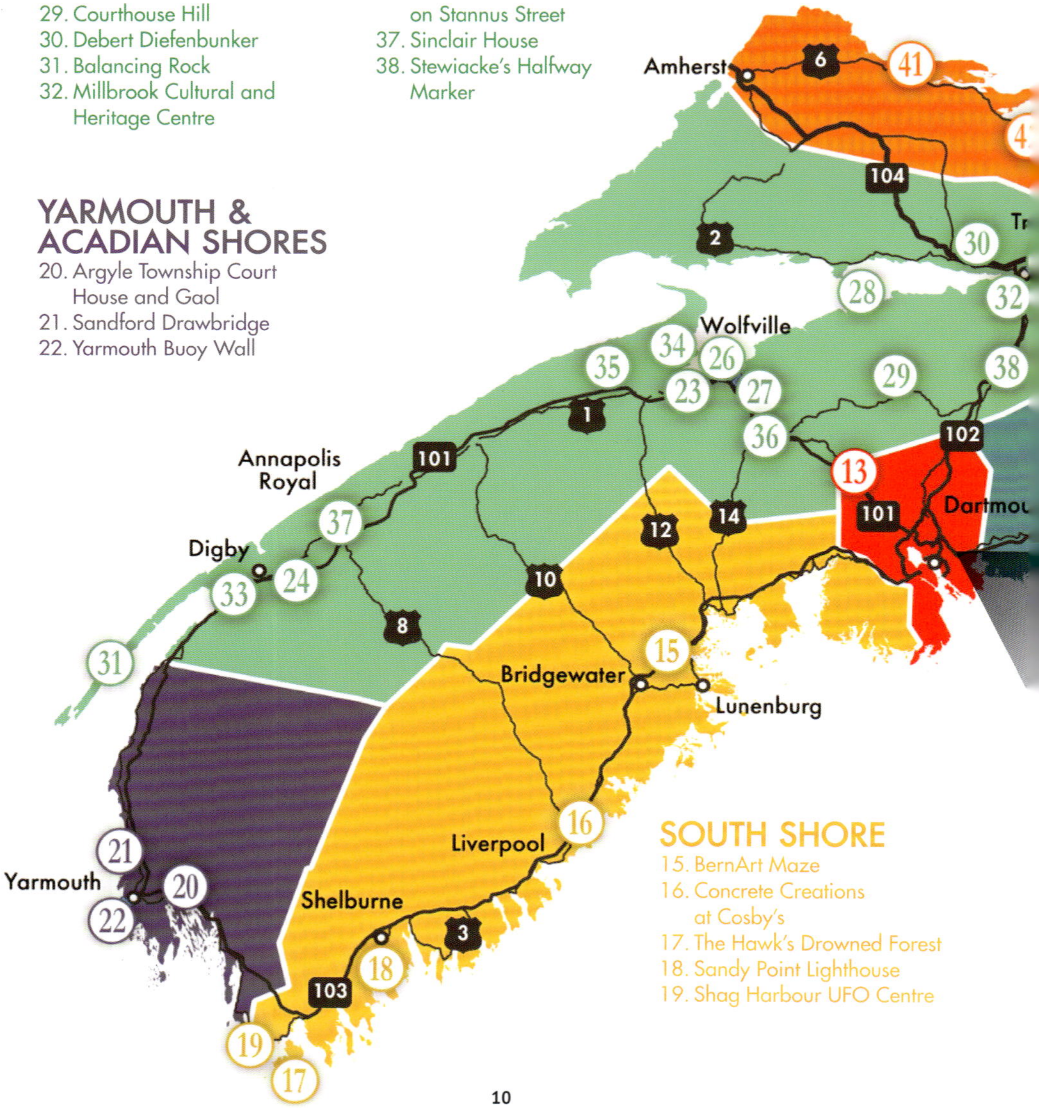

SOUTH SHORE

15. BernArt Maze
16. Concrete Creations at Cosby's
17. The Hawk's Drowned Forest
18. Sandy Point Lighthouse
19. Shag Harbour UFO Centre

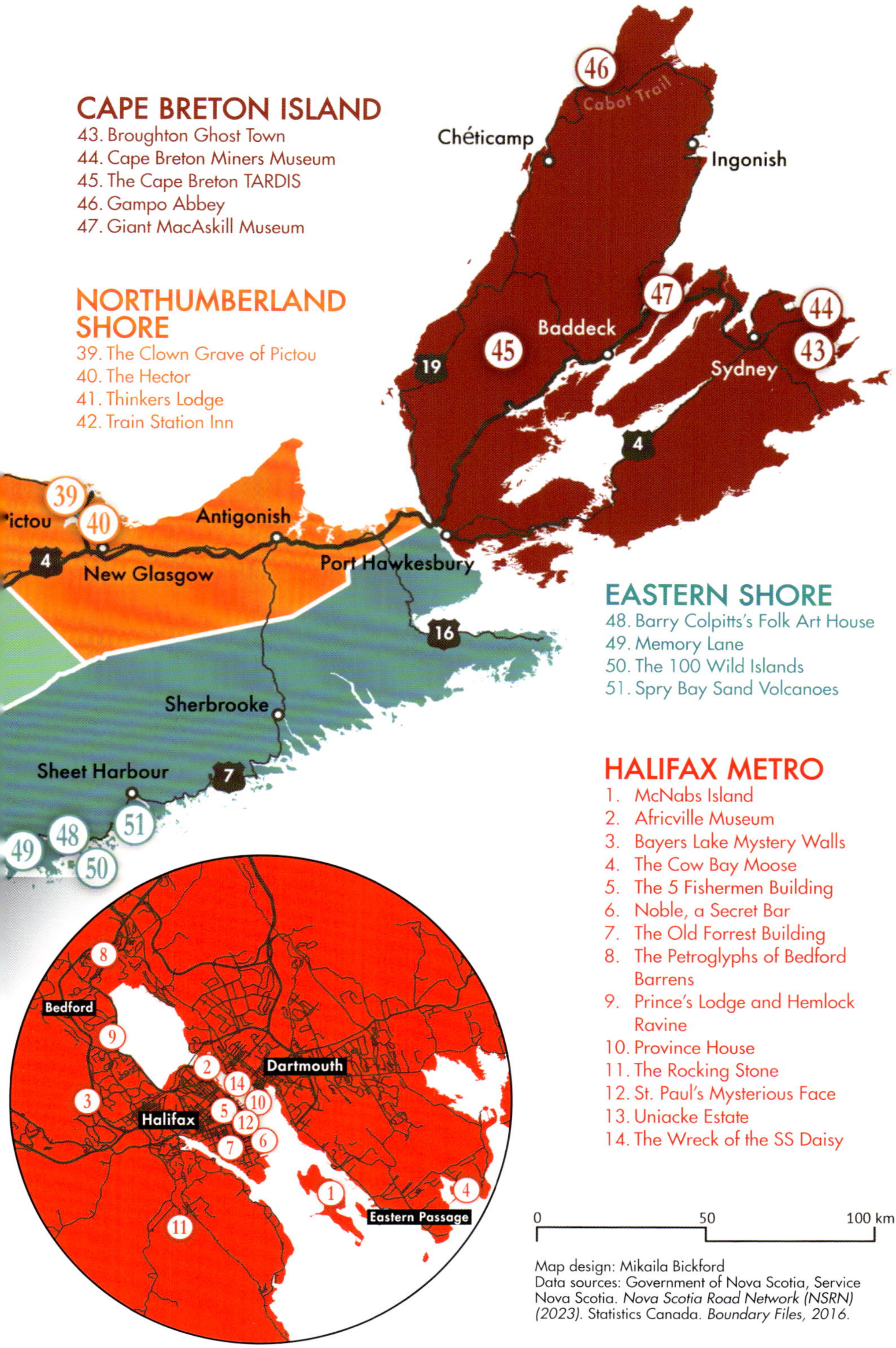

Map design: Mikaila Bickford
Data sources: Government of Nova Scotia, Service Nova Scotia. *Nova Scotia Road Network (NSRN) (2023)*. Statistics Canada. *Boundary Files, 2016.*

INTRODUCTION

You may think you know Nova Scotia. After all, you've heard of Peggy's Cove, the location of the most famous lighthouse in Canada; perhaps you've even visited it. Or maybe you're Nova Scotian yourself, and kitchen parties and lobster dinners hold a special place in your heart. But whether you're a resident, a repeat visitor, or looking forward to your first trip to the province, there's more to experience than you ever imagined—if you're willing to venture off the beaten path.

This book covers a range of sites and interests, including nature, history, art, paleontology, architecture, social justice, the paranormal, sports, geology, transportation, government, and popular culture. Many spots are completely wheelchair accessible and perfect for those with small children, while others are a better fit for those who are able and willing to traverse more difficult terrain. No matter your age, ability level, and interest, there's an adventure that will speak to you in the pages that follow.

HOW TO USE THIS BOOK

Beyond Peggy's Cove is organized by the geographical regions defined by Tourism Nova Scotia. Listed clockwise around the province starting from Nova Scotia's capital, they are Halifax Metro, South Shore, Yarmouth & Acadian Shores, Bay of Fundy & Annapolis Valley, Northumberland Shore, Cape Breton Island, and Eastern Shore. Each site is plotted on the map on pages 10 and 11, for easy reference and planning.

Each entry consists of four sections: What, Where, Details, and Tips. The Tips section details important information for visiting:

Accessibility, Fees, Parking/Directions, and other notes, including online resources. All fees (and other online information) were accurate as of 2026 and are subject to change.

A world of wondrously unusual sights is waiting for those who venture off the tourist track in Nova Scotia. May this book inspire you to explore them.

Happy adventuring!

Stacy Ann Milford

LAND ACKNOWLEDGEMENT

We must acknowledge that we are in Mi'kma'ki, the ancestral and unceded territory of the Mi'kmaq people. The people of the Mi'kmaw Nation have lived on this territory for millennia, and we acknowledge them as the past, present, and future caretakers of this land.

We further acknowledge that people of African descent have shared these lands for over 400 years, and we honour their histories and contributions.

We recognize that without action, an acknowledgement is empty. It marks the beginning of the work ahead of us, not the end.

Let us continue to work together in peace and friendship.

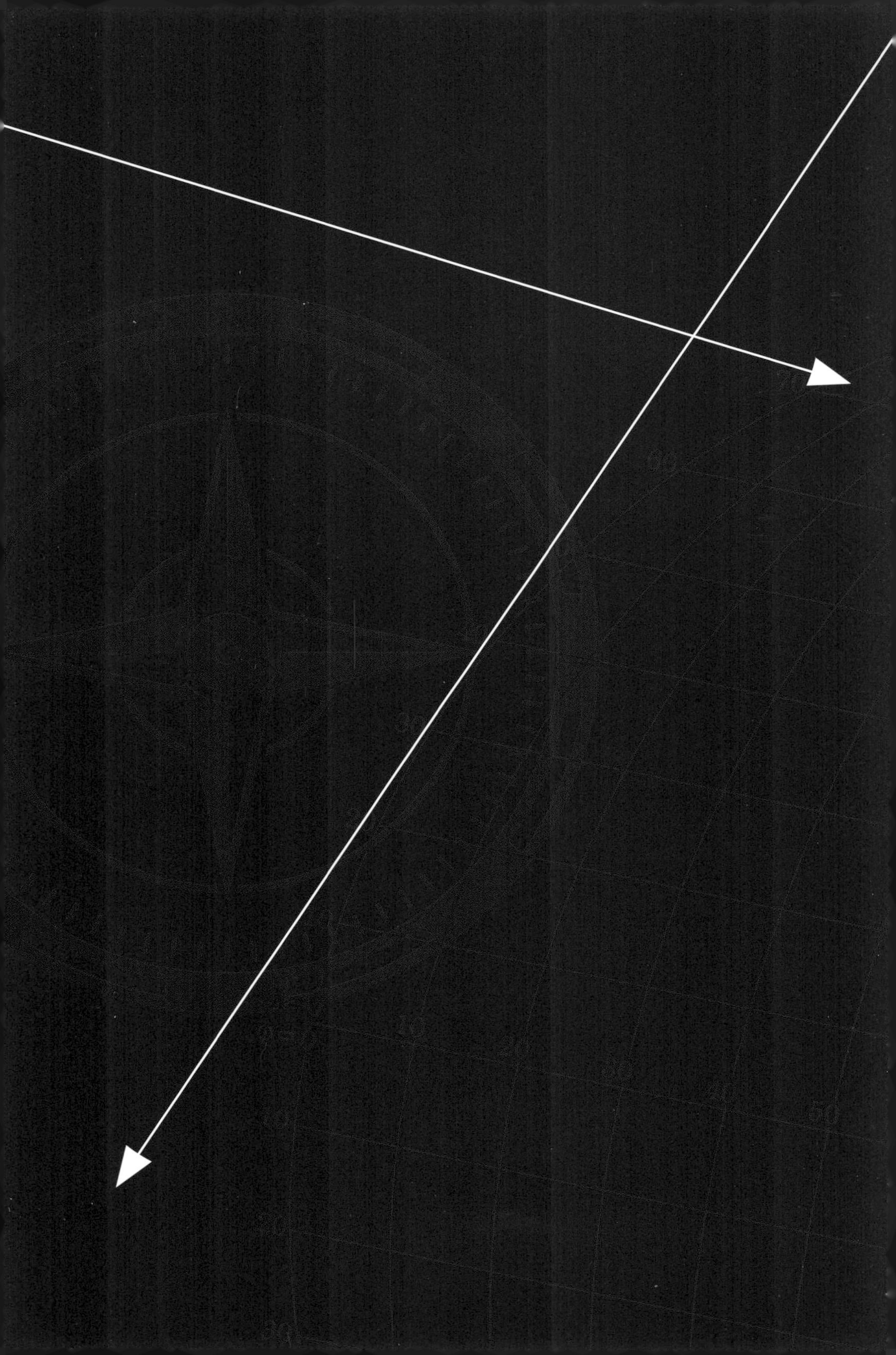

HALIFAX METRØ

Encompassing Halifax Regional Municipality's urban core (including Dartmouth, Halifax proper, and surrounding areas), Halifax Metro is the smallest geographical region covered in this book. But don't let its size fool you—this area boasts by far the largest population in Nova Scotia and contains a variety of unusual sites, all within easy reach of the provincial capital.

1 Abandoned McNabs Island

WHAT

An abandoned island in Halifax harbour featuring pristine natural beauty and historical ruins, which, unlike most of the other islands in the harbour, is open to the public.

WHERE

At the entrance to Halifax harbour (visible from Halifax and Dartmouth).

DETAILS

Several islands hide in plain sight in Halifax harbour, minutes from the bustling downtown core of Nova Scotia's capital. Over the nearly 300 years since Halifax was established, these islands have been home to a wide array of human activity and structures: settlements, prisons, lighthouses, cemeteries, quarantine facilities, military fortifications, and gallows. In 2026, most of these islands are off limits to the public, but that's not the case for McNabs Island, one of Halifax's true hidden gems.

McNabs Island, the largest island, is situated at the harbour entrance. Its history can be traced thousands of years to its use as Mi'kmaw hunting and fishing grounds. By the late 1600s, McNabs Island was a fishing centre used by the French. After mainland Nova Scotia was ceded to Britain, the island was privately owned, first by nephews of Edward Cornwallis (Halifax's founder), and then by Peter McNab (one of Cornwallis's lieutenants), who established tenant farms here.

The island's strategic location was not lost on the British government, and a variety of military fortifications were established

here starting in the 1800s. Over the years, the island was also home to a popular dancing and dining spot, picnic grounds, a soda pop factory, a teahouse, a beach where army deserters were hanged, a lighthouse (that once was housed in a military Martello tower), and a cholera quarantine site.

Largely abandoned since World War II, McNabs Island, despite its proximity to Halifax's urban core, now feels like a lost world. Its 4 square kilometres contain an intoxicating blend of pristine nature and historical remnants. Most of the island is a provincial park, although Fort McNab National Historic Site is managed by Parks Canada. Over 200 species of birds make their homes here, along with coyotes, rabbits, deer, and other animals. Hiking trails crisscross the island, providing visitors access to tranquil stone and sand beaches, wooded areas, marshland, and panoramic views.

Fort Ives and Fort MacNab can both be explored (exercise caution, as with any abandoned site), and visitors can walk past long-abandoned residences and imagine what life on the island was like decades ago.

Of the two cemeteries on the island, one is a cholera cemetery from the 1800s, the other the McNab family plot within Fort McNab. Wreck Cove contains several marooned vessels, some of which are visible on the beach at low tide.

McNabs Island is accessible only by water. If you don't have your own boat or kayak, you can charter a boat from Fisherman's Cove (Eastern Passage), which will take approximately 15 to 20 minutes, or from Halifax, a slightly longer journey. The Friends of McNabs Island Society, dedicated to promoting and preserving the island, includes contact information on their website for local boat operators. The society also offers guided tours to the island from Fisherman's Cove in the summer.

ACCESSIBILITY: The island is not wheelchair accessible and features rough terrain.
FEES: None for the island itself, but unless you have your own boat transportation, you'll need to hire a local boat operator. Round-trip boat transportation to the island from Fisherman's Cove or Halifax usually costs $20 to $25 per person; contact the boat operators by phone or email to arrange transportation.
PARKING/DIRECTIONS: The island can be reached only by boat; parking at tour boat operators' premises will vary.
MORE: Even in the summer, bringing layers of clothing is a good idea, since it can be windier and colder on the island than on the mainland. Visit mcnabsisland.ca for more information.

2 Africville Museum: Telling a Story of Oppression, Community, and Solidarity

WHAT

The reconstructed church (and heart) of Africville, a community of Black Nova Scotians founded in the 19th century and destroyed by the City of Halifax in the 1960s.

WHERE

5795 Africville Road, Halifax.

DETAILS

Many visitors—and even Halifax residents—haven't heard of Africville and aren't aware that enslaved people laboured to build much of Halifax in the 1700s. There's evidence that early Black settlers, formerly enslaved people, and Black Loyalists may have lived in the area that became Africville, on the shores of the Bedford Basin. By the 1800s, when Africville was officially founded, it was a vibrant, close-knit community for Black Nova Scotians, for whom it was a haven from the racism they faced in Halifax.

Over its 150-year existence, Africville was a small, open-door community on the northern edge of Halifax. There were residences, stores, a post office, a dance hall, a school, local businesses, and a Baptist church, which served as the centre of the community. Although residents paid taxes, the City of Halifax repeatedly denied them basic services such as running water, electricity, paved roads, sewage disposal, garbage collection, police services, and a cemetery. The City placed a variety of undesirable or dangerous services in Africville over the years, including a fertilizer plant, slaughterhouses, a prison, an

View overlooking the back of Seaview African United Baptist Church, Africville circa 1965.

infectious diseases hospital, a railway with speeding trains, and toxic, medical, and human waste dumps.

Africville, rezoned as industrial land in 1947, eventually became known to many Halifax residents as a slum built by squatters, even though Africvillians held employment, paid taxes, and cared for their land and homes. In the 1960s, the City of Halifax decided to raze the community and relocate residents—about 400 people—rather than provide proper services (despite a public meeting during which residents voted against relocation).

Africville's destruction took five years. Residents were often given only a few hours' notice before their houses were destroyed. In some cases, homes were demolished while their owners were out, without their knowledge or permission. The Seaview United Baptist church, the heart of the community, was razed in the middle of the night. Structures disappeared daily, and many families were transported to their new homes via garbage trucks or dump trucks when a moving company set up by the City cancelled. Residents were promised housing in Halifax, but they found that their housing deals never actually materialized, or that they fell short of what was promised, forcing many to leave the province or to turn to welfare to continue to live in Halifax. Africville's last home was demolished in 1970.

Despite the immense challenges, Africvillians shared a strong sense of community spirit and mobilized over the years to fight various

ACCESSIBILITY: The museum itself is wheelchair accessible; the adjacent park features crusher-dust pathways.

FEES: Admission is charged to visit the museum, but the grounds are free; open year-round. If the museum is closed, you can scan the QR code next to the door and follow the free Walking Africville Audio Tour, narrated by former residents. Adults: $10 / Students/Seniors (55+): $9 / 5 & under: free

PARKING/DIRECTIONS: Ample free on-site parking.

MORE: Visit africvillemuseum.org for more information.

injustices. The Africville Genealogy Society was created in the 1980s to fight for compensation for the community's destruction. It took decades, but a settlement was reached, and in 2010 the City of Halifax officially apologized to the residents of Africville. Settlement funds were used to rebuild the community's beloved church, which now serves as the Africville Museum, where visitors can learn about the tragic yet inspiring history of the community. The surrounding area is now a park (and National Historic Site of Canada) with informational plaques, while other parts of the former Africville were turned into ramps for the MacKay Bridge, the Fairview Container Terminal, and private housing.

Africville is an important reminder of the oppression Black Nova Scotians have faced and continue to face and a symbol of the remarkable sense of community and solidarity of Africvillians in the struggle against racism.

3 Bayers Lake Mystery Walls

WHAT

Mysterious 200-year-old stone ruins that defy identification, within a busy commercial area.

WHERE

Off Lovett's Lake Court, next to Chain Lake Drive (surrounded by Bayers Lake Business Park), Halifax.

DETAILS

Hidden within a small, overgrown tract of forest surrounded by the bustling Bayers Lake Business Park lies a mystery made of stone.

Several mysteries, to be more accurate. As implausible as it seems for an area nestled between busy highways, the ruins of a five-sided structure, a 3-foot-high stone wall stretching 200 metres, and a stone staircase to nowhere are scattered throughout this tiny section of woods. The ruins are of ironstone slate and were assembled without mortar. Are these the remains of a Viking settlement? Early military fortifications? Perhaps something more mundane, like a sheep pen? It seems the jury's still out.

Bayers Lake Mystery Walls were discovered in the 1980s, when development of the area was accelerating. Due to the rugged forest terrain and the site's location in the centre of a busy commercial district, a full archaeological excavation has proven impractical. However, more than one archaeological group has tackled this enduring enigma, and the site has been researched over the years. Unfortunately, efforts thus far have proven largely inconclusive.

Testing of the moss on the stones has dated the ruins to the late 1700s or early 1800s, but any recovered artifacts are much too modern to offer any clues to the site's original purpose. No evidence of fire has been found, which would seem to rule out a domestic dwelling. Similarly, soil tests haven't shown elevated levels of phosphorus, typically an indicator of human activity such as animal husbandry. And no documentation of the site exists in historical records, which would seem to rule out a defensive fortification.

Whatever their original purpose, the Bayers Lake Mystery Walls are vulnerable to vandalization and are now protected by the Nova Scotia Special Places Act.

ACCESSIBILITY: The site is not wheelchair accessible and features rough forest terrain.

FEES: None; can be accessed year-round.

PARKING/DIRECTIONS: There is a 1.5-kilometre "trail" to the site, but the paths are overgrown, unmarked, strewn with boulders, and, in places, nearly impossible to find. The easiest way to discover the ruins is to park at the end of Lovett Lake Court, and find the picnic table area to the right of the building at the end of the road (90 Lovett Lake Court). You'll see the path into the woods behind the picnic tables, which leads directly to the five-sided structure and takes only a few minutes. To locate the wall, go to the far end of the structure on the right side and head to the path that leads down a slope. Stay to the left at the fork, and then when the path branches into three, take the middle path; within a few minutes, you'll emerge at the wall.

MORE: Disturbing the stone remains is prohibited, as is digging or taking anything from the site, and trail cameras ensure that this centuries-old mystery is preserved for future generations.

4 The Cow Bay Moose:
A Relic in Concrete

WHAT

A giant concrete moose sculpture that is the last remaining vestige of a collection of concrete beachside animals created by Winston Bronnum, a well-known Canadian folk artist.

WHERE

1287 Cow Bay Road, at Silver Sands Beach Park, Cow Bay.

DETAILS

Moose are not a common sight in Halifax Regional Municipality. However, there's one place where you are guaranteed a moose sighting: at Silver Sands Beach Park in Cow Bay.

This towering 12-foot-tall specimen was created out of concrete in 1959 by folk artist Winston Bronnum, a former construction worker who channelled his self-taught carving and sculpting skills into fashioning larger-than-life animals as landmarks and roadside attractions. The Cow Bay Moose was initially part of a larger collection at Silver Sands Beach featuring various concrete beachside animals, all created by Bronnum.

With its fine white sand, Silver Sands Beach was popular with beach-lovers hailing from the local area and even Dartmouth and Halifax from the late 1800s to 1960s. The beach, which used to extend from the Cow Bay Moose to Hartlen's Point, had an on-site dance hall and canteen. However, about a decade after the animal sculptures made their debut, the City of Halifax removed all the sand to use in construction projects, effectively destroying the beach and exposing the rocks you see today.

The beach's popularity waned, and eventually the animals fell into ruin, leaving the Cow Bay Moose as the last vestige of the concrete zoo.

If this antlered behemoth seems familiar, it could be because you've seen some of Bronnum's other works. He created Jumbo the Elephant in Ontario, as well as several sculptures in New Brunswick: Blowhard the Broken-Down Racehorse, the Maugerville Potato, Gladstone Horse, and the World's Largest Lobster (which, contrary to popular belief, isn't the world's largest lobster—that honour goes to a gargantuan lobster sculpture in Qianjiang, Hubei province, China).

ACCESSIBILITY: The Cow Bay Moose site is fully wheelchair accessible.

FEES: None; can be accessed year-round.

PARKING/DIRECTIONS: A small free on-site parking lot.

MORE: It's tough spending six decades by the sea, constantly exposed to the elements. In recent years, the Cow Bay Moose had faded into an odd orange shade, and Nova Scotia artist Lynda McConnell volunteered to revamp his appearance with a new paint job in 2014. She returns yearly for touch-ups, leaving the venerable moose looking as good as new. His appearance in the TV series *Trailer Park Boys* in 2006 cemented his place in local history, and he even has a fan club: Friends of the Moose.

5 The 5 Fishermen Building:
Halifax's Haunted Historic Morgue

WHAT

A morbidly historic building that was the city's first funeral home and served as the mortuary for victims of the *Titanic* and the Halifax Explosion, it is now a restaurant with a reputation for paranormal activity.

WHERE

1740 Argyle Street, Halifax.

DETAILS

The 5 Fishermen is a beautifully renovated restaurant and cocktail lounge that gives little indication of its fascinating macabre past. The building sits across from Halifax's oldest building (St. Paul's Anglican Church) and dates to 1817. In the last two centuries, it has served various roles in the local community. It initially opened its doors as a school with close ties to the nearby church, providing free education to even the poorest children in Halifax, the first school in the country to do so.

Later, the building was purchased by Anna Leonowens, the teacher who founded the Halifax Victorian School of Art and Design. If her name sounds familiar, it may be because her previous experiences as a governess to the king of Siam's children were made into the Broadway musical and movie *The King and I*, based on a book she penned. Leonowens's art school eventually outgrew the space and became the Nova Scotia College of Art and Design. It's after her departure that the building's history takes a ghoulish turn with the arrival of the Snow family, who ran a successful mortuary.

Coffins outside Snow & Co. Undertaker for victims of the Halifax Explosion, 1917.

Snow & Company Undertaker, the city's first funeral home, played a role in two of the greatest global disasters of the early 20th century. When the RMS *Titanic* sank off the coast of Newfoundland in 1912, Halifax was the closest mainland port, and it was from here that rescue operations were carried out. John Snow took over 100 coffins out to the site of the disaster and buried many of the bodies at sea, but the wealthiest victims,

including John Jacob Astor IV, were brought back to the funeral home for arrangements to be made. Five years later, Snow & Company Undertaker was called in again, after the Halifax Explosion killed over 2,000 people and injured another 9,000. The blast shattered the windows of the funeral home, but the Snow family still conducted services for dozens of victims daily, about 2,000 in all, with rows of coffins lined up outside the building.

It's no surprise, then, that paranormal sightings abound, reported by both staff and patrons (even those who aren't aware of the building's history). Glasses that fly off shelves, taps that turn themselves on and off, cold spots, whispered voices, and foggy apparitions moving up and down the staircase are all commonplace. But don't let that stop you from visiting: staff insist whatever presence remains in the building is mischievous, but harmless.

ACCESSIBILITY: The restaurant is wheelchair accessible.

FEES: None to enter; the restaurant is open year-round.

PARKING/DIRECTIONS: No on-site parking, but limited paid street parking and paid parking lots (including Prince George Hotel, Scotia Square Parkade, and Nova Centre) are located nearby.

MORE: Staff are willing to talk about their paranormal experiences in the building, so be sure to ask. Visit fivefishermen.com for more information.

6 Noble:
Halifax's Secret Bar

WHAT
A secret underground speakeasy for which a password is required.

WHERE
1563 Barrington Street, Halifax (beneath The Middle Spoon Desserterie & Bar).

DETAILS
Without the secret password, you'll never gain entry to Halifax's secret bar. Worse, staff won't even acknowledge that it exists.

That's how seriously protocol is observed at Noble, the subterranean speakeasy concealed beneath The Middle Spoon Desserterie & Bar. Guests who aren't in the know eat their desserts on the main level without even realizing there's a whole other world under their feet. If you do know the password phrase that changes weekly (and say it correctly), you'll be escorted to the basement, through a labyrinth of corridors to a huge metal door. Beyond, Noble awaits, in all its Prohibition-era splendour.

Wall-to-wall books line one wall, while another is adorned with red velvet curtains, portraits, and tufted leather seating. Candle-lit tables and eclectic vintage-style chairs are scattered across the room, and an upright piano against one wall awaits a player. Jazz music from bygone decades plays softly.

You can order from the same vast dessert menu offered upstairs, but the drink menu is exclusive to Noble. Don't see anything you like out of the dozens of creative, and delightfully named, cocktails on offer? Just speak to the bartender, who can make any drink you can imagine.

The swanky-yet-comfortable surroundings, secret password, and hidden underground location all lend Noble a clandestine air of exclusivity that's unique in Halifax and beyond. So, what's the coveted secret password? That's, well, a secret. But intrepid rum-runners should poke around The Middle Spoon's website, and you just might stumble upon a clue that will put you in the know.

ACCESSIBILITY: There's no elevator on the property, and there are over a dozen stairs to reach the basement level through the restaurant. But you can contact staff to gain entry via the side door, which has significantly fewer steps. Alternatively, for visitors with physical limitations, staff can make the extensive cocktail menu from the Noble available to you in The Middle Spoon, which is at street level.

FEES: There is no entry fee. Noble is usually open Thursday, Friday, and Saturday nights from about 7 or 8 p.m. until the wee hours of the morning.

PARKING/DIRECTIONS: No on-site parking; use nearby paid parking lots or paid street parking.

MORE: If the green cactus in The Middle Spoon's window is lit, that's the signal that Noble is open. Visit themiddlespoon.com for more information.

7 The Old Forrest Building: L.M. Montgomery's Stomping Grounds

WHAT

The stately building where L.M. Montgomery studied English literature for a year and which later served as the model for Redmond College in her famous books featuring Anne Shirley.

WHERE

Dalhousie University's Carleton Campus, 5869 University Avenue, Halifax (at University Avenue and Robie Street).

DETAILS

Anne of Green Gables, and by extension her world-famous creator Lucy Maud Montgomery, are synonymous with Prince Edward Island, where the author was born and raised and set many of her iconic novels. But there's an important Nova Scotia connection to Canada's beloved red-headed orphan and her trailblazing author that might surprise you.

The Forrest Building on University Avenue opened in 1887 and once comprised the whole of Dalhousie University, then called Dalhousie College. L.M. Montgomery was a student of English literature there from 1895 to 1896. She could afford to study only for a year, which in itself was an accomplishment, since few women at that time attained post-secondary education, and even her home community did not support her education goals. While Montgomery was on campus, she published her work in the school newspaper, *The Gazette*. She returned to live in Halifax from 1901 to 1902, when she worked for *The Daily Echo*.

Montgomery's short time in Nova Scotia must have made an impression on her, because she wrote about Halifax, fictionalized as the town of Kingsport, and many of its landmarks in her novels (specifically, *Anne of the Island*). The Old Burying Ground appears as "Old St. John's Cemetery." Point Pleasant Park, to which the author retreated when she was homesick for PEI, is mentioned as an unnamed park. "St.

John's Street" is a clear reference to Barrington Street. And Dalhousie University itself inspired the novel's Redmond College, where Anne of Green Gables—if not Montgomery herself—completed her Bachelor of Arts degree.

The Forrest Building is now home to Dalhousie Faculty of Health's nursing, physiotherapy, and occupational therapy programs. But you can visit the lobby to see the plaque that formally recognizes the building's connection to one of Canada's best-known authors and imagine L.M. Montgomery wandering these halls in pursuit of higher education—and maybe a kindred spirit or two.

ACCESSIBILITY: The Forrest Building is wheelchair accessible.

FEES: None; the building can be visited year-round.

PARKING/DIRECTIONS: While parking permits can be obtained if you're a student or faculty, parking is otherwise challenging. Visitors can use the metred parking on nearby streets or public parking lots.

MORE: L.M. Montgomery fans can also swing by the building where she worked as a journalist, now The Old Triangle Irish Alehouse on Prince Street, as well as the Barrington Street and Church Street neighbourhoods where she once lived.

8 The Petroglyphs of Bedford Barrens

WHAT

Sacred Mi'kmaw rock carvings from hundreds of years ago, within a Bedford subdivision.

WHERE

Along a footpath through the woods that begins at the end of Emmerson Street, Bedford.

DETAILS

At the end of a quiet residential street in Bedford, an unobtrusive footpath leads to a sacred Mi'kmaw site featuring pre-contact rock carvings—and most Bedford residents have no idea they're even here.

Much better known are the Mi'kmaw petroglyphs at Kejimkujik National Park and National Historic Site, in southwest Nova Scotia; it's one of the largest petroglyph collections in eastern North America, but only one of the sites is accessible to visitors, and only by guided tour. The Bedford site, by contrast, can be visited at any time by anyone able to walk up a short hill.

Within an area of about 2 square metres are two stone carvings, or petroglyphs, etched into the quartzite that makes up the Bedford Barrens. Both glyphs lie beyond an interpretive panel that sheds light on the history of the carvings and reproduces clearly the figures etched into the rock. The larger petroglyph consists of a circle surrounding an eight-pointed symbol—likely a star, an important and ancient symbol for the sun in Mi'kmaw spirituality, and one used today as a key design element and a cultural symbol among the

A MI'KMAW
Elapskita'sikl kun'tew-iktuk etekl msit tami Mi'kma'ki. Ekinua'tekekl aqq ekina muekl ta'n ki's sa'q telo'ltisni'k aqq tel-lukutisni'k L'nuk'k Mi'kma'kik. Newte'jk maqamikew ta'n etekl, na Kwepe'k
Tapu'kl Elapskita'sikl, ukmuljin el-kini'skwikit kloqoej aqq l'nu, na maw-wl-nenmumkl ta'n etekl tett. Kwepe'k na kepmite'tasik aqq l'nue'l pekitnawetumkewe'l ika'tasikl wjit kniskamijinaqi'k. Etaweyek mu tala'tunew ula pekitnawetumkewe'l mita iknmatimkewe'l na wjit kniskamijinaqi'k
Kwepe'k etek senusaqtuneke'l Asoqmapskiaj. Kwepe'k na wiaqtek Kjipuktuk, aqq we'kaw Pitue'k Kjipuktuk. Wejkwa'taqnik Kwepe'k kepmite'tasik aqq keknuite'tasik. Kwepe'k i'-tl-mawita'mkis wejkwa'taqnik (19th aqq 20th kaskimtlnaqnipunqekewe'l). Kwepe'k etek wejuowk puljainewawti pemiaq kikjuk Asoqmapskiaj, na wjit welteksip etl-ktuknimk wjit L'nu'k ta'n elta'jik Kjipuktuk atankua'titl pu'taliewe'l aqq piluey koqoey kisitu'titl.
L'nu'k ne'kaw kepmite'tmi'tij Kwepe'k, katu atel 1980'sek pilue'k wenik Nopa Sko'sia poqji-nenmi'tisn Elapskita'sikl. 1990'sek poqji-naskwa'tasikip maqamikew kikjuk Kwepe'k wjit ewi'kamk, toqo kaqi-ksika'tu'tisoq Elapskita'sikl. Mawita'snik wenik kulutmnew wli-anko'tasiktn aqq kepmite'tasiktn ula maqamikew. Na kisa'tu'tis Kwepe'k tlui'tasiktn Kmitkinaqewey Kepmite'tasik Maqamikew 1994ek.
Me' ne'kaw kiskuk wejiaq ta'n teli-anko'tasik tplutaqn-iktuk. Tplutaqn teluisik Nopa Sko'siaewe'l Kepmite'tasikl Maqamikewil.
Pjilita'q, welta'sualulek pejitaioq ula tetuji kepmite'tasik maqamikew aqq etaweyek ankaptmnew aqq ankite'tmnew koqoey nemituoq, katu kisi-pkwatu'n mukk sama'tu koqoey.
Wela'liek
Wela'liek

ACRED PLACE
re found throughout the
and recording Mi'kmaw life
e at the Bedford Barrens.
and an abstract human
zed petroglyphs at the site.
te and a place where
e offered to honour our
e respect these offerings, as
dge of the Bedford Basin,
uktuk," or the Great
of Halifax Harbour. The
place during the early
Barrens were close to the
; an ideal camping area for
sans, as they journeyed to
pecial place to the Mi'kmaq,
to the wider community
e 1990s, when the land
zoned for development,
oglyphs, several groups
ection. This eventually led
g a National Historic Site of
ler the Nova Scotia Special
place and ask that you look,
o disturbance behind.
On trouve les pétroglyphes, ou gravures sur pierre, partout dans la région de Mi'kma'ki. Ils sont le reflet du mode de vie et de l'histoire des Mi'kmaq. L'un de ces endroits est ici même, à Bedford Barrens.
Deux illustrations, une étoile à huit pointes et une figure humaine abstraite, constituent les pétroglyphes les plus faciles à reconnaître sur le site. Bedford Barrens est un site spécial où des objets de valeur culturelle sont offerts en hommage à nos ancêtres. Nous prions les visiteurs de respecter ces offrandes, qui sont présentées en guise de cadeaux.
Situé sur la crête sud-ouest, le bassin de Bedford fait partie du Kjipuktuk ou le Grand-Hâvre, un secteur qui inclut tout le port d'Halifax. Bedford Barrens était un endroit important du début au milieu du XXe siècle. Les landes étaient situées près de la gare de Bedford, ce qui en faisait un lieu de camping idéal pour les vanniers et les artisans Mi'kmaq, qui se rendaient à Halifax vendre leurs produits.
Pendant longtemps, ce site a été un endroit spécial pour les Mi'kmaq; or, les pétroglyphes n'ont été portés à la connaissance du public que pendant les années 1980. Durant la décennie qui allait suivre, lorsque le terrain entourant Bedford Barrens a été zoné pour l'aménagement, constituant ainsi une menace possible pour les pétroglyphes, plusieurs groupes ont exercé des pressions pour que ce lieu sacré soit protégé. Grâce à leurs activités, Bedford Barrens est devenu un lieu historique national du Canada en 1994 [Lieu historique national du Canada des Pétroglyphes-de-Bedford].
Ce lieu continue d'être protégé en vertu de la Special Places Protection Act de la Nouvelle-Écosse.
Nous vous accueillons dans ce lieu sacré et nous vous invitons à regarder, à toucher et à vous abonner à la réflexion sans déranger quoi que soit.
Wela'liek

Mi'kmaq. The second glyph resembles an abstract humanoid figure. Both petroglyphs appear to have been made with stone tools and therefore are likely over 500 years old.

The petroglyphs at the Bedford Barrens became a National Historic Site in 1994, about a decade after the carvings were identified by a local and brought to the attention of the wider Nova Scotia community. The site is sacred to the Mi'kmaq, who wanted to keep the petroglyphs in their natural form to be enjoyed by visitors until the elements inevitably erode them beyond recognition. The trail was later redirected around the site so that hikers wouldn't walk on the carvings, which are protected under the Nova Scotia Special Places Protection Act.

ACCESSIBILITY: The short gravel forest path is on an incline.

FEES: None; can be accessed year-round.

PARKING/DIRECTIONS: Park on Emmerson Street. Drive to the end of Emmerson Street, and on your left by a small opening in the woods, you'll see a rock with a commemorative plaque marking this as a Mi'kmaw heritage site. Follow the gravel footpath for about a minute (around 60 metres): the site is on your left, just off the path, with an interpretive panel in Mi'kmaq, English, and French. The petroglyphs can be difficult to spot, depending on lighting conditions. Stand at the interpretive panel; both petroglyphs are on the rock face ahead and to the left.

MORE: Hanging from the trees around the carvings, you'll likely see colourful offerings placed as gifts to Mi'kmaw ancestors. Visitors are asked to respect these offerings and not to disturb the site.

9 Prince's Lodge Rotunda and Hemlock Ravine Park:
Vestiges of an 18th-Century Estate

WHAT

A park featuring old-growth hemlocks, a heart-shaped pond, and remnants of an 18th-century country estate with royal connections.

WHERE

Hemlock Ravine Park and heart-shaped pond: 40 Kent Avenue, Bedford. Rotunda: Approximately 499 Bedford Highway (roughly opposite Kent Avenue, on the opposite side of the highway).

DETAILS

Once a playground for Halifax's wealthy elite and a favourite of the lieutenant-governor, Hemlock Ravine Park and environs (aptly named Prince's Lodge) look a little different nowadays.

In 1780, a country villa was built on this spot for Nova Scotia lieutenant-governor John Wentworth. Fourteen years later, Prince Edward, Duke of Kent (later father to Queen Victoria), came to Halifax with his beloved mistress, Madame de St. Laurent, to command the garrison. He loved the estate so much that Wentworth lent it to him. The Duke and his mistress resided at Prince's Lodge for six years, during which time Edward channelled his love of landscape design and architecture into revamping the estate grounds. Ornamental temples, lavish gardens, waterfalls, and a grotto were added and served as the setting for a variety of social activities for the elite of the time.

By the early 1800s, the estate had been vacated, and it soon fell into disrepair. The Duke's grandson, Prince Arthur, arrived in 1869

and turned the oval pond created by his grandfather into the heart-shaped pond of today, to commemorate the love shared by the Duke and Madame de St. Laurent.

Today, the City of Halifax owns the 200-acre grounds, but all that's left of the original estate is the heart-shaped pond (a favourite with local ducks and the romantically inclined) and one lone ornamental temple: the rotunda, sitting on a hill overlooking the water. Built in 1796, it's one of the last Georgian buildings in the area. Its round dome and elegant columns symbolize a bygone era, quite out of place perched beside the busy Bedford Highway.

Yet another reason to visit Hemlock Ravine Park is the old-growth forest, where 300-year-old hemlock trees can soar to a height of 80 feet. Because the area was protected as a private royal estate and not logged to supply trees to the garrison (not the case for the rest of the city), the park remains one of the few places to reconnect with untouched nature and to see plants and animals you're unlikely to see anywhere else in Halifax.

ACCESSIBILITY: Most of the trails in Hemlock Ravine Park are suitable for wheelchairs, as is the trail around the heart-shaped pond. The rotunda itself, while it can easily be viewed from several vantage points, cannot be reached by wheelchair.

FEES: None.

PARKING/DIRECTIONS: Hemlock Ravine Park is at the end of Bedford's Kent Avenue. A free parking lot is on the left, just before the dead end. The heart-shaped pond is beside the parking lot.

The rotunda is visible from Prince Street, but the best view is from Bedford Highway. There's no designated parking for the rotunda itself, as there's no entry into the structure. For intrepid adventurers who want a closer look, the rotunda is on a hill across Bedford Highway, behind a guardrail and past a set of train tracks.

MORE: For more information on the history of the site, turn right on Prince Street just before you get to the park—there's a small green space with an informative plaque that includes illustrations of what the estate looked like hundreds of years ago.

10 Province House:
Canada's Oldest Seat of Government

WHAT

The oldest legislative building in Canada, now a National Historic Site open to the public.

WHERE

1726 Hollis Street, downtown Halifax.

DETAILS

The historic setting of the oldest seat of government in Canada is completely free to visit—and it's gloriously grand.

Province House is where the Nova Scotia House of Assembly meets to debate and pass laws and has done for over 200 years. This imposing edifice, built between 1811 and 1819, owes much of its elegance to the influence of the classical architecture of Greece and Rome. However, local details, like the fish-shaped entrance door handles, are a clear nod to life in the Maritimes.

The grandeur begins as soon as you step inside, with black-and-white marble tiles in the central hall, leading to the grand staircase with its cast-iron balustrades and Ionic columns. Continue into the Legislative Assembly, where, if you visit when the House of Assembly is in session, you can witness government proceedings in action.

The highlight of a tour at Province House, at least for a book lover, is the Legislative Library. Once the Supreme Court of Nova Scotia's chamber, the room became a library in the 1860s and a number of changes were made, including the addition of a mezzanine balcony and a library ladder. The graceful, curving twin staircases are accompanied by ornate metalwork, and portraits and busts keep lucky readers company. Its oldest book dates to 1488.

The Red Chamber is the one area of Province House that has changed little since the 19th century. Once the meeting place for the Legislative Council, it is now used mostly for receptions, meetings, and ceremonies (and, in the case of the thrones, for visiting royalty). With magnificent hand-crafted ornamentation on the walls and fireplace, you'd be hard-pressed to find a more elegant room in the city. Don't forget to look up—the remarkable Palladian plaster and stucco work on the ceiling is unique in Canada.

ACCESSIBILITY: There is a wheelchair-accessible entrance at the back of Province House, and the building is completely wheelchair accessible.

FEES: None; except for statutory holidays, Province House is open weekdays year-round.

PARKING/DIRECTIONS: No on-site parking. Some paid street parking is available around Province House; read parking signs carefully to avoid being towed.

MORE: Visitors can do a self-guided tour of the building or observe a sitting of the House of Assembly or the proceedings of a committee, when in session.

Upon entering the building, you'll need to show a photo ID. You'll also go through a metal detector, and any belongings with you will pass through an X-ray machine for security—any belongings that can't enter may be picked up when you exit. Visit nslegislature.ca/get-involved/visit-province-house for more information.

11 The Rocking Stone: A Geological Celebrity

WHAT

A geological marvel that was one of the province's first tourist attractions.

WHERE

Kidston Lake Park, Spryfield.

DETAILS

If asked to name Nova Scotia's oldest tourist attraction, most people would probably guess the Halifax Citadel or perhaps one of the province's many historical lighthouses. But a major contender for the title of oldest tourist site in the province is actually a rock that has been enticing visitors for more than 200 years.

The Kidston Lake Rocking Stone, located within the Halifax community of Spryfield, is a massive granite boulder estimated to weigh several hundred tonnes and measures 6 metres long, 4 metres wide, and nearly 3 metres tall. Rocking stones, also known as logan stones, are large rocks that are so precariously balanced on their unstable bases that they can be moved back and forth with little force, sometimes with just a touch. Spryfield's specimen, according to the Geological Survey of Canada, could lay claim to being the biggest rocking stone on earth.

Experts say that the boulder originated several kilometres northwest of its current site, where, thousands of years ago, it eroded from the surrounding granite bedrock and was picked up by a glacier, which melted and dropped the stone in its current position.

Likely the most studied rock in Nova Scotia, the Rocking Stone was

Rocking Stone, circa 1895.

first documented in 1823, at which point Halifax's *Acadian Recorder* noted that even a child could set it rocking with the touch of a hand. According to lore, in the late 1800s a group of soldiers rocked the local landmark with such force that it became more stable and more difficult to move. Over the years, debris accumulated beneath the rock, further reducing its rocking capability. Once Kidston Lake Park was developed around the Rocking Stone and foot traffic increased accordingly during the 1980s and 1990s, the base of the rock was worn down even more, until finally the massive stone lost its ability to rock altogether.

The Spryfield community became involved in the 1990s, cleaning away the accumulated debris and rendering the famous boulder once again rockable, albeit with the aid of a lever. The stone and the park in which it sits were granted heritage status by the Halifax Regional Municipality in 2022, giving Rocking Stone some protection against future development, and hopefully allowing it to be preserved for future generations.

As of 2026, there isn't a permanent lever and recent official attempts to rock it have not been successful; locals insist that the Rocking Stone can be rocked—if you have the right tool and skills.

ACCESSIBILITY: The gravel paths to the Rocking Stone are wide and not extremely steep, but they can be uneven or muddy.

FEES: None; can be accessed year-round.

PARKING/DIRECTIONS: Free on-site parking. You can park at the end of Fieldstone Street, where the path to Kidston Beach begins. Alternatively, drive through the gate at the end of the street to another parking area slightly closer to the Rocking Stone. From there, take the gravel path to the left (Kidston Lake will be visible on your right). After a few minutes, the trail will branch into three pathways; the left and centre paths both lead to the Rocking Stone, which you'll see ahead in a clearing.

MORE: During the Victorian era, the Rocking Stone became a favourite haunt of Halifax picnickers, who travelled there to enjoy a packed lunch while sitting atop the geological curiosity, gently rocking all the while.

12 St. Paul's Mysterious "Face in the Window"

WHAT

Halifax's oldest building, containing two haunting remnants from the Halifax Explosion.

WHERE

1749 Argyle Street, Halifax (at the south end of the Grand Parade, opposite City Hall).

DETAILS

As the oldest building in Halifax, and the first Anglican church to be built in North America, St. Paul's Church has seen its share of history since it was built in 1750, the year following the establishment of the city. Perhaps its most intriguing feature is the mysterious "face in the window," a relic from the 1917 Halifax Explosion.

The collision of two ships, one a munitions ship bound for the frontlines of World War I, in Halifax harbour in December 1917 resulted in the world's biggest human-made pre-atomic explosion. Thousands died, and thousands more were injured, either from the blast itself or from the tsunami that followed. The city was devastated, and the blast was felt as far away as Cape Breton and Prince Edward Island. Miraculously, St. Paul's Church survived—in fact, it was used as an emergency hospital and morgue for victims of the explosion—but not without a few scars.

When you enter the church, you will notice a piece of steel—reportedly an airborne piece of framing from a window that was blown out of a nearby building during the explosion—embedded high up on

the wall in the vestibule above the War Memorial Arch (the inner door of the church). A sign indicates that it's a relic from the explosion. Less obvious to the casual observer, however, is the church's mystery window, featuring the profile of a human face. Even though it is more striking when viewed from the inside of the church, it can also be seen from the exterior if you walk along Argyle Street; look for the third set of windows from the north end of the church, and you'll see what looks like a man's profile in the upper right pane.

The origins of this oddity are shrouded in mystery and vary depending on who you talk to. The most probable explanation is that, although most windows in the church were obliterated by the explosion, this particular window shattered in the shape of a human head, and the shards were later preserved by the church as a relic of the explosion. The outline could conceivably result from heat-related discolouration or residue left by the blast.

Other legends have gained popularity. Is the silhouette that of the church deacon who was standing in the gallery at the moment of the explosion, when the intense heat forever etched his profile onto the glass? Or, more morbidly, perhaps it's the result of the decapitated head of a sailor flying through the air forcefully enough to shatter the glass cleanly in the shape of his silhouette? As far as the congregation of St. Paul's is concerned, the mystery profile resembles Reverend Jean-Baptiste Moreau, a missionary who arrived in Halifax with Cornwallis and served at the church until 1753, going on to help found the town of Lunenburg.

Whatever its origins, the mysterious window has been intriguing visitors to St. Paul's for over a century. Not that it's the only reason for a visit to the church: St. Paul's Georgian architecture, as well as the royal pew, crypt, stained glass, pipe organ, mural tablets, heraldic devices, and other artifacts and memorials, commemorate over 250 years of life in Halifax.

ACCESSIBILITY: The church is wheelchair accessible.

FEES: None; all tours are free, but the church welcomes donations. Guided tours conducted by students are typically offered from June to October; simply walk in and ask if guided tours are available. There isn't a fixed schedule, so if you are looking for a guided tour, contact the church in advance to set up a tour.

Self-guided tours with explanatory pamphlets are possible on weekdays throughout the year. Check online or contact staff for up-to-date hours. It's best to call ahead if you're visiting off-season, as the main doors might be locked, even when the church is open.

PARKING/DIRECTIONS: Parking in downtown Halifax can be a challenge, but there are metred street parking spots, paid lots, and parkades nearby. The church is easily reached on foot from the waterfront and other tourist spots in central Halifax.

MORE: This is a functioning church; although visitors are welcome to join church services, self-guided tours should only be conducted during the hours outlined by the church. Visit stpaulshalifax.org for more information.

13 Uniacke: A Preserved Country House Estate

WHAT

A historic Georgian neoclassical mansion preserved with its original contents and extensive grounds containing English landscape features rarely seen this side of the Atlantic Ocean.

WHERE

758 Nova Scotia Trunk (Highway) 1, Mount Uniacke, half an hour from downtown Halifax.

DETAILS

It's hard to believe this sprawling, elegant estate with its imposing pillars, portico, and lakeside trails was once a summer home.

Built between 1813 and 1815, Uniacke Estate was a country house for Richard John Uniacke, a lawyer, politician, and attorney general of Nova Scotia. Uniacke named his estate after his ancestral home in Ireland (Mount Uniacke), which he left at age 20, after an argument with his father, to try his luck in the New World. The architecturally significant house was built in the Georgian neoclassical style—one of the best remaining examples of this style in the country—and was owned by seven generations of the same family until the house and its contents were sold to the province in 1949. In stark contrast to most other heritage properties, everything here is original to the house: the mahogany furniture, portraits, wood stoves, and even Uniacke's books in the library.

The imposing mansion is only part of the story. Uniacke eventually acquired 11,800 acres of land, which he tried to farm, with limited

success, as the soil is among the poorest in the province. He did have some luck growing turnips, and inventive turnip recipes from the period survive (several of these are online at the Nova Scotia Archives, including one for turnip wine). Today, 2,500 acres of land remain as part of the estate, much of it almost unchanged—in fact, this is one of the last surviving examples of English landscape garden design left in North America. Visitors can also see the recessed barrier, or ha-ha,

Uniacke created to contain his sheep without obstructing the view; it's one of only two ha-has left in the entire country. The seven walking trails have informative plaques on the history of the landscape, including a path along peaceful Lake Martha (named for Uniacke's wife).

Uniacke Estate would have been hard to miss 200 years ago if you were travelling on what was then Nova Scotia's only road, the Post Road, between Halifax and Windsor. Sections of the original road remain as part of the estate's trail system. Of note inside the house are the original, massive fireplace in the basement kitchen (now the tearoom and gift shop), the curved wall in the hallway on the second floor that encompasses several closets, and cat access holes in closet doors.

ACCESSIBILITY: The first floor of the house is wheelchair accessible (there's a ramp at the back), but the second floor and the tearoom and shop in the basement are not. One of the forest trails is also wheelchair accessible.

FEES: Admission is charged to enter the house, which is open from June to October; the grounds and trails are free and open year-round. Adults: $3.90 / Seniors (65+): $2.80 / Youth (6–17): $2.80 / Children (under 6): free

PARKING/DIRECTIONS: Ample free on-site parking.

MORE: Take a few minutes to explore the barn, one of the few original outbuildings remaining on the property, with its antique carriages and sleighs. Visit uniacke.novascotia.ca for more information.

14 The Wreck of the SS *Daisy*: Dartmouth's Mystery Ship

WHAT

The rusting remains of a 100-plus-year-old British navy trawler that now forms part of the Dartmouth shoreline.

WHERE

Along the Dartmouth shore, in the shadow of the Macdonald Bridge, off Windmill Road.

DETAILS

The waters of Halifax harbour obscure the remains of more than 40 ships, lost to time beneath the waves and sediment. But one mystery ship is plainly visible beneath the MacDonald Bridge—though most of the people who travel over the bridge daily are unaware of the vessel's existence. This is the SS *Daisy*, whose rusting hull has been a fixture of the Dartmouth shoreline for decades.

While retirement has not been kind to *Daisy*, she had an illustrious career. Built in Scotland in 1911, *Daisy* initially served as a trawler for Britain's Royal Navy. She arrived in Canada after World War I, having been purchased by the government of Newfoundland, which was not yet part of Canada. From there, *Daisy*'s resume becomes even more interesting.

Her next role was that of a police boat—to enforce Prohibition and hunt rum-runners off the coast of St. John's, Newfoundland. *Daisy* was docked at the town of Burin in 1929 when an earthquake with a magnitude of 7.2 on the Richter scale struck the Grand Banks, and she was able to aid in rescue efforts when the resulting tsunami struck the Burin Peninsula, rescuing stranded victims and helping to save boats and

SS *Daisy* in the days of rum-running and smuggling.

houses that had been swept out to sea. In the mid-1940s, a Dartmouth construction and dredging company, J.P. Porter, bought *Daisy* to use as a tugboat. A few years later, she was decommissioned, filled with dirt and rocks, and unceremoniously sunk into Halifax harbour, becoming part of Dartmouth's shoreline over the years as the shore was extended.

Daisy is not the only scrapped piece of maritime history in the harbour; there are multiple vessels slowly rotting away along the Halifax and Dartmouth shores. Ships of *Daisy*'s age were built to last, and last they have, although they're now mere shells of their former glory.

ACCESSIBILITY: The route to *Daisy* is not wheelchair accessible and involves navigating overgrown, uneven terrain.

FEES: None.

PARKING/DIRECTIONS: The waterfront land where *Daisy* rests is owned by the City, and the best way to spot her is from the water, in a kayak or on a boat tour, just beyond the Macdonald Bridge. Land access is trickier. Some have had success approaching via Shore Road, while others have been turned away by construction workers who didn't want visitors walking on private property to get to the ship.

Locals often walk their dogs along the train tracks from Jamieson Street to the bridge, and while it's possible to access *Daisy* using this route, be aware that this is trespassing.

MORE: *Daisy*'s 80 years in Halifax harbour have taken a toll, and it may be unsafe to venture onto her rusted skeleton. It is safer to view *Daisy* from the water or from the shoreline adjacent to what remains of her hull.

Visitors should be aware that this is not the most picturesque part of town, though it does provide a fascinating glimpse into Dartmouth's industrial past.

HALIFAX SHIPYARD
ASSEMBLY HALL

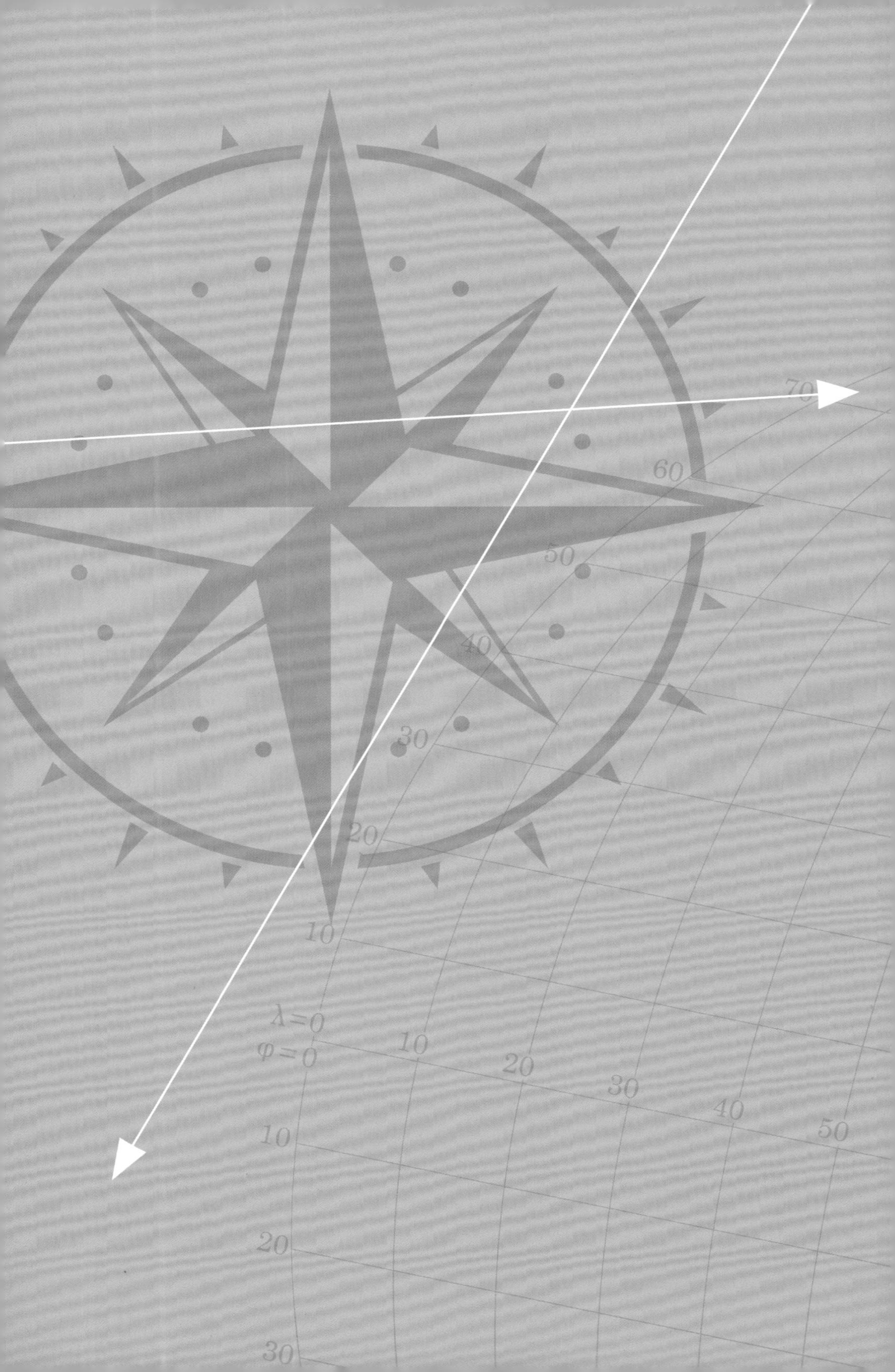
70
60
50
40
30
20
10
λ=0
φ=0
10
20
30
40
50
10
20
30

SOUTH SHØRE

Some of Nova Scotia's most iconic scenery is found along the South Shore. This is the land of rugged granite shores, picturesque lighthouses, colourful coastal towns, and quaint fishing villages. This region also contains surprising off-the-beaten-path sites that have to be seen to be believed.

15 BernArt Maze: Canada's First Art Maze

WHAT

Canada's first art maze, comprising almost a kilometre of winding walls, fantastical creatures, and whimsical murals made from recycled and found objects, created by volunteer artists from around the world.

WHERE

1136 Highway 325, Blockhouse (a few minutes from Mahone Bay).

DETAILS

"Get lost." It's not typically something you'd thank someone for saying to you. But in the case of BernArt Maze, you just might—getting lost is the key to exploring a quirky, fanciful world of artistry and make-believe unique not only in Nova Scotia but also in Canada.

German-born artists and entrepreneurs Bernd and Nicole Krebes arrived in Nova Scotia in 2002 and started a tiling business. In 2012, Bernd decided to make his long-time dream of building a maze a reality. It took six years to bring his vision to life.

BernArt Maze, the country's first art maze, consists of almost a kilometre of whimsical, art-filled, maze-like outdoor pathways created mostly from recycled and found items. This once empty piece of land close to Mahone Bay and Lunenburg was transformed with the help of volunteer artists from all over the world, and it's now a one-of-a-kind, ever-evolving, open-air art project that visitors love to get lost in.

You'll encounter a velociraptor poised to attack, a cave adorned with "prehistoric" cave paintings, and a huge shark emerging from a wall, open mouth full of rows of menacing teeth. A mermaid perches on a

raindrop-shaped wall cutout; an adorable multiple-eyed alien watches your progress. There are fantastical painted murals, a passthrough with hundreds of china teacups and saucers embedded in cement walls, floor, and ceiling, and beautiful mosaics made of stone, tile, and coloured glass.

BernArt Maze is a riot of colour and imagination, with surprises at every turn. Allow the playful sculptures to draw you along the path to see what's around the next corner, or sit for a spell on one of the many quirky benches and be inspired by the uplifting quotations along the walls.

You could spend as little as half an hour in the maze. Or, if you're taking the time to explore every nook and cranny and maybe enjoying a picnic lunch at one of the outdoor tables, you could easily spend several hours here.

The maze is always changing, and an extension is in the works, including an enchanted forest, bounded by a massive wall of lobster traps. You can't miss the entrance to the maze—a gargantuan spider stands guard above it.

ACCESSIBILITY: The maze is wheelchair accessible.

FEES: Admission is charged; open seasonally, from June until Thanksgiving. Adults: $12 / Children (4–12): $10 / Children 3 & under: free / Season Ticket: $16

PARKING/DIRECTIONS: Follow the signs for BernArt on Route 325; drive past the storage units to the free parking lot.

MORE: There's an on-site porta-potty. Visit bernartmaze.ca for more information.

16 Concrete Creations at Cosby's Garden Centre

WHAT

A whimsical concrete wonderland hiding in the forest behind a garden centre.

WHERE

4122 Sandy Cove Road, Nova Scotia Trunk 3, Brooklyn.

DETAILS

In Nova Scotia, you don't need to head to a museum to enjoy masterfully carved sculptures—sometimes an artistic experience is as close as a local garden centre.

Concrete Creations started when local sculptor (and owner of Cosby's Garden Centre) Ivan Higgins made concrete sculptures to display plants. From there, his creative talents led to the fabrication of 60-plus sculptures scattered throughout the 3.2 hectares of old-growth forest behind the garden centre.

The sculptural wonderland brought to life by Higgins's imagination and skill includes a stone dragon about to take flight, an ethereal castle above a beautiful cascade of colourful plants, startlingly realistic acrobats in mid-performance, giants in repose, a jester waiting for you to pose beside him, and countless animals peeking from the foliage. Visitors with sharp eyes will be rewarded—many of the concrete sculptures are well hidden.

Higgins works on his magical creations each winter, progressing from pencil drawings to wire forms to completed concrete pieces. As he often receives commissions from businesses and individuals,

don't be surprised if you see his work throughout Nova Scotia and beyond. Take a quick stroll behind Cosby's Garden Centre to see a few prominent sculptures or spend considerably longer meandering along the forest trail.

ACCESSIBILITY: Trails and paths are stable, wide, and comprised of gravel, grass, and wood chips, making them accessible for most visitors, although there are some slight inclines.

FEES: None; visitors are invited to donate to a fund dedicated to maintaining the sculptures (look for signs along the trail). Concrete Creations is open year-round—even when the garden centre is closed, the trails behind it are accessible.

PARKING/DIRECTIONS: Free on-site parking.

MORE: Craving more concrete magic? Sign up for a creative concrete workshop, held every January at Cosby's Garden Centre.Visit concretecreations.info for more information.

17 The Hawk Beach's Ancient Drowned Forest

WHAT

A white sand beach featuring an ancient drowned forest, a mysterious buried structure, birding opportunities, and a view of the province's tallest lighthouse.

WHERE

The southern tip of Cape Sable Island, off New Road.

DETAILS

The southernmost tip of Nova Scotia boasts more than its share of delightfully unusual features, including a drowned forest from over 1,000 years ago that is revealed only at low tide.

The Hawk Beach, located on Cape Sable Island (not to be confused with Sable Island), is a treat for visitors who take the time to travel here. Known colloquially as "The Hawk," it's a 20-minute drive south of Barrington, reached via the Cape Sable Island Causeway, but it feels a world away from the mainland. Definitely a contender for the most beautiful beach in the province, The Hawk's rocky shore gives way to white sands that stretch toward turquoise water, bringing to mind the waters of the Caribbean, in colour if not water temperature.

Low tide reveals the remains of a 1,500-year-old drowned forest, its ancient stumps and freshwater peat exposed on the ocean floor twice a day. Hundreds of eerie, misshapen stumps dot the beach, draped with seaweed and trailing long-dead root systems. They date to a time when the sea level was several metres lower than it is now. As sea levels continue to rise due to climate change, the beach gets pushed back farther and farther, exposing more ancient tree stumps and eroding those closest to the sea.

More than 100 shipwrecks are located off Cape Sable Island, and in fact, The Hawk is named after a schooner that washed ashore in the 1800s. Look for the remains of a structure, likely from the 18th century, that stick mysteriously out of the sand. Archaeologists have suggested that the structure may have been a wharf or fishing stage, but other suggestions have included everything from a cattle pen to a Viking fortification.

Birders will want to flock to The Hawk—as part of the Cape Sable Important Bird Area, it's hard to find a better place for birdwatching in the province, and the endangered piping plover is just one significant birding population that can be viewed here. Visitors can also glimpse Cape Sable Lighthouse, the tallest lighthouse in Nova Scotia, from the beach. For an even better view, drive to the end of Fish Plant Road, where there's plentiful parking and the best view you'll get of the lighthouse without being in a boat.

ACCESSIBILITY: The beach is not wheelchair accessible and features stones and an incline down to the water.

FEES: None; can be visited year-round.

PARKING/DIRECTIONS: Once on Cape Sable Island, follow Hawk Point Road. Turn left onto New Road, and drive to the free parking lot at the end. At the beach, walk to the right to find the drowned forest. You can also park along the road leading to the official lot, which will bring you closer to the ancient stumps.

MORE: Check tide times, as the drowned forest is revealed only at low tide.

18 Sandy Point Lighthouse and Its Disappearing Sandbar

WHAT

One of the oldest wooden lighthouses still standing in Nova Scotia, notable for a sandbar that allows visitors to walk out to the lighthouse at low tide.

WHERE

1586 Sandy Point Road, Shelburne.

DETAILS

At high tide, the Sandy Point Lighthouse appears to float gracefully on the waters of Shelburne harbour. But six hours later, visitors can walk out to this 19th-century relic—sometimes without getting wet. This beautiful spot is little known outside Shelburne, so you may even have it all to yourself.

Located on an idyllic spit of light sand tinged with shades of pink and purple and surrounded by crystal-clear water, the lighthouse's location is picture-perfect. The soft sand is perfect for collecting sand dollars (if they're dark brown, purple, or red, they're still alive and should be left where they are; dead ones have been bleached white or light grey by the sun). At or around low tide, it only takes a few minutes to stroll out to the lighthouse; if you get the timing is right, you may barely get wet, but prepare for shallow water and wet sand. It's not possible to enter the lighthouse itself, but you can walk all the way around the outside.

The first lighthouse at Shelburne harbour was built in 1873 on a timber pier marking the entrance to the harbour, near the location of the current lighthouse. This first iteration burned down a few years later; it was rebuilt, likely around 1880, on the same pier. By 1903, the ocean had wreaked havoc on the foundation of the wooden pier, and the lighthouse was moved to its current site, to mark the sandspit. The ocean continues to take a toll on the lighthouse, and renovations have been carried out over the years to keep this nearly 150-year-old structure looking its best.

Historically, lighthouse keepers lived onshore on the site of what is now the Shelburne community centre and would walk or row, depending on the tide, out to the lighthouse every night to turn on the light, and every morning to turn it off. When the lighthouse became automated in the 1980s, a lighthouse keeper was no longer needed. Although the lighthouse was decommissioned in 1999, the light is still operational and can be seen from almost 20 kilometres away. While it may not serve the crucial navigational purpose it once did, the lighthouse remains an important symbol for local fishermen and the entire community.

ACCESSIBILITY: A grassy park and boardwalk on site offer reasonably accessible viewing points; walking to the lighthouse requires wading into the ocean, navigating rocks, and walking on sand.

FEES: None; can be viewed year-round.

PARKING/DIRECTIONS: Free on-site parking.

MORE: The on-site community centre operates a canteen that offers beverages and snacks during the summer months, and the adjacent park has a seating area and picnic tables. On select dates in the summer, the centre also offers full breakfasts; check online for details. Visit facebook.com/SandyPointLighthouseAndCommunityCentre for more information.

⑲ Shag Harbour UFO Centre and Crash Site

WHAT

A museum that commemorates Canada's best-documented UFO sighting; the alleged crash site is just down the road.

WHERE

5615 Highway 3, Shag Harbour.

DETAILS

Ghost ships, sea serpents, and hidden pirate treasure are the tall tales you might expect to hear along Nova Scotia's South Shore—not alien encounters. Yet it was a UFO sighting that put the tiny fishing community of Shag Harbour on the map more than 50 years ago.

On the night of October 4, 1967, numerous residents noticed flashing orange lights in the sky, which quickly dove toward the ocean, finally seeming to hover on the water itself, less than a mile from shore. The lights slowly

disappeared. Assuming that an airplane had crashed, people reported the incident to the RCMP—several officers themselves saw the lights—and the Coast Guard. In all, dozens of credible witnesses saw the incident.

Divers searched the crash site for days without finding any evidence (at least, any evidence revealed to the public) except yellow foam left behind by the unidentified craft. No civilian or military aircraft were reported missing that evening, prompting the Rescue Coordination Centre to list the incident in a report to the Canadian Forces as being of "unknown origin."

Over the years, different theories have been proposed for the sighting and lack of evidence, including claims that an alien ship was retrieved by the military at their secret base half an hour away, and then covered up (there was indeed a joint secret US-Canadian military base near Shelburne, built to track Soviet submarines during the Cold War). Some people claimed that a second UFO arrived to aid the first, before both craft broke the surface of the ocean and flew away. All we know for sure is that officials on site confirmed that something had hit the water that night and that it wasn't a flare or any known aircraft, and they had no idea what it was.

Science fiction? Reality? Or something in between? Whatever the truth may be, the Shag Harbour Incident Interpretive Centre commemorates this mysterious crash with newspaper articles, documentaries, memorabilia, and a gift shop.

ACCESSIBILITY: The museum is wheelchair accessible.

FEES: Admission is charged; open seasonally from June to September. Adults: $10 / Children (5–12): $5 / Children under 5: free

PARKING/DIRECTIONS: Free on-site parking. Drive a few minutes west of the UFO Centre on Nova Scotia Trunk 3 to a large sign and gazebo marking where the craft allegedly crashed.

MORE: Serious UFO fans may want to attend the annual Shag Harbour UFO Conference held in late September or early October. Visit shagharbourincident.ca for more information.

RBOUR OVNI

N
W
E
S

YARMOUTH AND ACADIAN SHORES

Acadian, English, and Mi'kmaw cultures make up the rich fabric of the Yarmouth and Acadian Shores. It's here you'll find the biggest Acadian population in the province and maybe even hear French spoken by residents descended from settlers who came to the area from France hundreds of years ago.

20 Argyle Township Court House and Gaol

WHAT

Canada's oldest courthouse and gaol and the site of notorious trials with connections to some of the best-known public figures of the 1800s.

WHERE

8168 Highway 3, Tusket (just east of Yarmouth).

DETAILS

This simple yet elegant wooden building in the small fishing community of Tusket is the nation's oldest surviving courthouse and gaol. It's also the site of notorious trials from days gone by and has connections to some of the best-known public figures of the 1800s. It's now a National Historic Site operating as a museum.

Built in 1805, the Argyle Township Court House and Gaol served as a courthouse and gaol for nearly 145 years before becoming a municipal office in 1945. One of its most infamous cases was that of local murderer Omar P. Roberts, who was incarcerated here and became the last person ever to be hanged in the county. Author Thomas Chandler Haliburton served as Supreme Court judge, and famous political figures Sir Charles Tupper and Joseph Howe both gave campaign speeches on site.

Visitors can tour the courtroom, which remains little changed since the 1870s; the uncomfortable jury benches, prisoners' docket, and judge's podium are all original. The prison cell block on the lower level, used for prisoners whose offences ranged from debt to murder, is also original. Guests are free to step inside the dank, cramped, windowless

CANADA'S OLDEST
COURT HOUSE & GAOL
1805
E TRIBUNAL ET PRISON
PLUS ANCIEN AU CANADA

cells and close the heavy iron doors behind them to imagine the unenviable life of a 19th-century prisoner.

While it's been many years since court was held on site, or felons awaiting trial huddled in the tiny underground cells, this building remains important to the community of Tusket and now serves as the archives for the municipality of Argyle.

ACCESSIBILITY: The site is not wheelchair accessible—doorways are narrow, floor levels change suddenly, and steps are located throughout. Visitors who can climb a few steps can access the gift shop, which has a seating area. Staff have previously used an iPad to show virtual tours and photos of exhibits to guests with physical limitations.

The Archives building next door, however, is fully wheelchair accessible.

FEES: None; admission is by donation. Open seasonally from June to October.

PARKING/DIRECTIONS: Free on-site parking is available.

MORE: A guided tour is highly recommended, but self-guided audio tours are also offered in English and French. Visit argylecourthouse.com/court-house-museum for more information.

㉑ Sandford Drawbridge: Canada's Smallest Drawbridge

WHAT

A tiny, working drawbridge in an idyllic fishing village; it's Canada's smallest drawbridge and also one of the smallest in the world.

WHERE

47 Sandford Wharf Road, Yarmouth.

DETAILS

Blink, and you might miss the tiny drawbridge at the picturesque Sandford Wharf.

One of the ubiquitous lovely fishing communities that dot the shores of Nova Scotia, the tiny community of Sandford is about a 15-minute drive north of Yarmouth. Colourful seaside shacks, fishing boats, buoys, and lobster traps provide the perfect setting for this unexpectedly appealing drawbridge.

The Sandford Drawbridge has been rebuilt and moved several times since its original construction in 1915. Today, it connects the two sides of the Sandford Wharf, allowing both visitors and local fishermen and -women to cross the narrow channel quickly and easily. It also allows boats to pass through when it's open. Closed, it forms an inverted-V, and visitors can walk up one steep side of the bridge and down the other.

This iconic drawbridge holds a place of honour among locals as the world's smallest working drawbridge. While this distinction is not undisputed (another contender is the Somerset Bridge in Bermuda), it seems that the Sandford Drawbridge is, at the very least, the smallest working drawbridge in Canada.

103356

ACCESSIBILITY: Sandford Drawbridge is not wheelchair accessible, as there's no ramp, and visitors must climb steep sides with raised wood pieces serving as steps. However, the drawbridge can easily be viewed from the area around the wharf.

FEES: None; can be accessed year-round.

PARKING/DIRECTIONS: There is no official parking area, but it's easy to find a spot to pull over to enjoy the view or take a walk in the salty sea air.

MORE: Sandford Drawbridge looks quite different depending on whether you visit at low or high tide. This is an excellent location from which to watch the sun set. Visit sandforddrawbridge.ca for more information.

㉒ Yarmouth Buoy Wall

WHAT

A cheerful, ever-growing collection of washed-up buoys on a massive lobster trap wall, an ode to Nova Scotia's fishing heritage.

WHERE

1110 NS-304, Yarmouth Bar; just before Cape Forchu Lighthouse, on the right-hand side of the road.

DETAILS

Nothing says "the Maritimes" like a collection of colourful buoys hanging from a lobster trap—except maybe an entire wall of them hanging from hundreds of lobster traps, which is what you'll find in Yarmouth.

Buoys have always played an important role in Nova Scotia's maritime heritage. While the look and feel of buoys have changed over the years, they continue to help fishermen and -women locate their nets or traps as they make their living on the ocean and are often passed down from generation to generation. The colours and designs on buoys are more than artistic whimsy—they're unique to the family or individual they belong to, making them easily identifiable by their owner and by others in the trade.

Located just down the road from Cape Forchu Lighthouse, one of the most photographed lighthouses in the province, the Yarmouth Buoy Wall is an eye-catching monument to the sea. It consists of hundreds of lobster traps and an ever-growing collection of buoys inherited by the current property owners, who discovered upon buying their property that rogue buoys continually wash up on shore. One day, they hung some

#yarborbuoywall

of the buoys on lobster traps—and immediately, the project attracted attention, as visitors pulled over and photographed the buoy wall.

This ever-growing attraction now serves as a cheery backdrop for photos taken by locals and tourists alike, as they celebrate special events such as graduations and weddings or pose for a vacation selfie. The property owners welcome visitors and can often be found chatting to passersby about the buoy wall, life on the Bay of Fundy, and Yarmouth's lobster fishery—one of the biggest and most lucrative in the country.

If you visit during the Christmas season, you'll find the buoy wall decked out with festive lights that can be seen across the harbour.

ACCESSIBILITY: The area around the buoy wall isn't paved, but it's a fairly flat stretch of gravel and grass.

FEES: None; can be viewed year-round.

PARKING/DIRECTIONS: Free on-site parking.

MORE: If you're in Nova Scotia during the holidays, you'll find that various communities across the province put up Christmas trees made of buoys and lobster traps. It's a maritime tradition, and the buoys often honour lost fishermen and -women or those who still make a living on the ocean.

Troy Crowley
2948C

N
W
E
S
70
60
50
40
30
20
10
λ=0
φ=0
10
20
30
40
50
10
20
30

BAY OF FUNDY AND ANNAPOLIS VALLEY

Nova Scotia's Bay of Fundy and Annapolis Valley region is huge and diverse. It's home to the highest tides in the world, world-class wineries, and the first European settlement in Canada. It also contains an impressive number of unusual sites that will make you see the province in a whole new light.

23 The Acadian Dykes That Transformed Nova Scotia's Landscape

WHAT

Extensive dyke systems—the earliest of which were constructed nearly 400 years ago by Acadians—that allowed settlers to reclaim thousands of acres of tidal-flooded salt marshes, turning the area into usable farmland and transforming the province's landscape forever.

WHERE

Low-lying coastal areas, primarily in the Annapolis Valley (Wolfville, Grand-Pré, Annapolis Royal).

DETAILS

It might not look like it, but when you stroll along one of Nova Scotia's coastal dyke trails, you're walking on a technological marvel almost 400 years in the making.

In 1605, France established the first permanent European settlement in Canada, at Port-Royal in Nova Scotia. French settlers called Acadians built thriving communities here and in other areas across the Maritimes and even into Maine. Starting in the 1630s, Acadians reclaimed coastal land for farming by building dykes; some of the earliest examples of dyke building in the province were in the Port-Royal and Grand-Pré areas. They then expanded their dyke building to other areas in Nova Scotia, including other parts of the Minas Basin and the Bay of Fundy.

Acadian dykes relied on two important elements. Levees—huge embankments or dyke walls made of timber, clay, and sod—stopped the tide from flooding the salt marshes, creating usable farmland. Tide gates (also called sluices or aboiteaux) installed at the bottom of the levees allowed rainwater to drain out of the newly created fields during low tide, with a valve that closed at high tide to prevent salt water from entering. In this way, the Acadians harnessed the nutrients of Nova Scotia's vast salt marshes, turning what was previously unusable land into fertile farmland.

By 1713, Nova Scotia was under British control. Acadians continued to farm their lands, living under British rule and claiming neutrality. But by the mid-1750s and the start of the Seven Years War, between France and England, the British determined that the Acadians were too much of a risk. When the Acadians refused to sign an oath of allegiance to the British Crown, a series of forced removals, spanning decades, began in 1755. During this "Grand Dérangement," or Great Upheaval, over 11,000 Acadians were deported from Nova Scotia by the British, their homes and crops burned, with thousands dying in the process.

Eventually, Acadians were allowed to return to Nova Scotia. Many did, though they were typically not allowed to resettle their original lands, as those had been inherited by new settlers loyal to Britain (frequently New England Planters, who added to the Acadians' dykes over the years). Acadian dyke building using traditional methods continued into the early to mid-1800s.

It's still possible to walk along Acadian-built dykes today. Many have been turned into public trails, and while they've been maintained and resurfaced over the years, at their core they're still the same structures built by Acadians.

Among the best spots to walk upon or view dykes in the province are:

Grand-Pré National Historic Site: While the extensive dykelands adjacent to Grand-Pré are still being farmed and therefore private property, the Harvest Moon trail connecting Grand-Pré with Fort-Anne National Historic Site in Annapolis Royal does pass along or beside the dykes. Alternatively, the View Park on Old Post Road at Grand-Pré (also called the Landscape of Grand-Pré View Park, 69-161 Old Post Road, Grand-Pré) offers expansive views of the dykelands and the stunning surrounding landscape.

Annapolis Royal Historic Gardens: The Dykewalk at Annapolis Royal Historic Gardens (441 St. George Street, Annapolis Royal) allows visitors to stroll on top of centuries-old Acadian dyke embankments, and it only takes 10 to 15 minutes.

Wellington Dyke: New England Planters had already extended existing Acadian dykes in the area when they built this dyke in the early 1800s. Almost 2 kilometres long, with a path running along the embankment, it's on Wellington Dyke Road, just outside Port Williams, and it's marked by a large blue sign.

Wolfville (Wickwire Dyke and Bishop-Beckwith Dyke): Two dykes are accessible from Wolfville harbour. You can access the Bishop-Beckwith Dyke at the end of Harbourside Drive; it runs along an Acadian dyke from the mid-1700s to a spot near the Port Williams Bridge (there's a small parking lot on the Port Williams side, just off Highway 358, with a viewing platform and interpretive panels, if you want to start here). The Wickwire Dyke, built in the early 1800s by New England Planters, is accessible from Kings County Rail Trail/Old Dike Lane and runs west for almost 5 kilometres.

ACCESSIBILITY: The Harvest Moon Trail is generally wheelchair accessible; it's hard-packed and flat, but parts may be gravel or uneven. View Park on Old Post Road is wheelchair accessible. The Dykewalk at Annapolis Royal Historic Gardens is a flat, roughly mown path along the dyke tops. You can easily see Wellington Dyke from the flat, gravel parking area, but the trail on the embankment is grassy and uneven. The same can be said for both Wickwire Dyke and Bishop-Beckwith Dyke—there are spots near the parking lots at the start and end of each where the dykes can be easily and accessibly viewed, but walking on the embankments involves uneven, grassy terrain.

FEES: None; trails and viewpoints are accessible year-round.

PARKING/DIRECTIONS: Each of the above sites has free on-site parking (although the parking area at Wellington Dyke is not a formal lot, but rather a section of roadside gravel).

MORE: The dykes originally built so ingeniously by Acadians centuries ago today protect Nova Scotia's communities, farms, and infrastructure, especially in the Chignecto Isthmus, which connects the provinces of New Brunswick and Nova Scotia. For over 300 years, the dyke system built by Acadians has protected the area from rising sea levels, but these aging dykes have increasingly come under threat due to much-needed repairs and weather events related to climate change. Currently, a severe storm could result in flooding to the Chignecto Isthmus, completely cutting Nova Scotia off from the rest of Canada and making it (albeit temporarily) an island. Both provinces are working to create solutions to improve existing dykes and to build new ones.

24 Bear River (L'sitkuk): The Tidal Village on Stilts

WHAT

A tidal village with an artistic vibe, on stilts, in an area traditionally occupied by the Mi'kmaq.

WHERE

Bear River, on the border between Annapolis and Digby counties.

DETAILS

Nova Scotia is brimming with picturesque villages, but none have quite the vibe of charming Bear River. It sits on a river of the same name, which serves as the border between Annapolis and Digby counties, effectively bisecting the village between them. As Bear River is a tidal river, rising and falling by 5 metres twice a day, just a few hours make a dramatic difference in the appearance of the village. At high tide, the village rises above the water on stilts; at low tide, the water recedes, revealing extensive mudflats and marshlands.

Bear River lacks fast-food restaurants, retail chains, and traffic lights, making this the perfect escape from the everyday. There's also no municipal government here, since the village is part of two different counties; instead, Bear River is run by volunteer committees.

Colourful, centuries-old buildings line the main street, vestiges of the village's prosperous ship-building days in the 1800s. Nowadays, shops and galleries feature local artwork, so if you're looking for a gift or souvenir that you won't find anywhere else, this is the place to shop. The slow pace of life here means that the artists and shop owners always have time to chat. Restaurants offer tasty, award-winning dishes.

Bear River First Nation is adjacent to the village of Bear River. Stop at the nearby Mi'kmaq Heritage and Cultural Centre to learn about the Indigenous history and culture of the area and see the first birchbark canoe built here in decades using traditional methods.

ACCESSIBILITY: The main route (Wharf Street, where you'll see the buildings on stilts over the river) is fairly flat but could involve traversing uneven ground. Wheelchair accessibility for specific venues in Bear River varies.

FEES: None; can be visited year-round.

PARKING/DIRECTIONS: Park on Clementsvale Road (limited street parking is available) for easy walking distance to all the village sights.

MORE: For the most iconic view of the village, drive around to the back of the local fire department on River Road. Visit bearriver.ca for more information.

25 The Berlin Wall Panels of Bible Hill

WHAT

Canada's largest collection of panels from the fallen Berlin Wall, hidden along a trail behind a college campus.

WHERE

Bible Hill, just outside of Truro.

DETAILS

If there were a prize for the most successful game of hide-and-seek by a memorial of global and historical significance, it would doubtless be awarded to the panels of the Berlin Wall in Bible Hill.

Erected in 1961 as a physical and ideological barrier between East and West Germany, the Berlin Wall is instantly recognized as a symbol of the Cold War. It restricted movement and emigration, separated families, and prevented workers in East Germany from carrying out their jobs in West Germany. When the 140-kilometre-long monument came down in 1989, demand for pieces of it was high. Panels were gifted or sold to individuals, organizations, and governments around the world—in all, over 240 are scattered throughout more than 140 countries. Although most of these panels of the Berlin Wall have been put on permanent display and treated as the historically and culturally significant memorials they are, it's a surprise to find six huge panels standing unceremoniously in an overgrown field outside Truro.

The six graffiti-adorned cement panels, each measuring 12 feet by 4 feet, were purchased in Germany and brought to Truro by a local businessman after the Cold War ended. Initially, the panels were

displayed in a vacant lot in the middle of town. After controversy about how best to display them, they were moved in 2011 to Dalhousie University's Agricultural Campus, where they now sit in a small field wedged between the Haley Institute Building and the Cobequid Trail, along the Salmon River.

ACCESSIBILITY: The Berlin Wall panels sit in a meadow without paved pathways and aren't wheelchair accessible. A narrow strip of paving stones was once placed between the panels, but it has not been maintained and has become overgrown and potentially uneven.

FEES: None; can be accessed year-round.

PARKING/DIRECTIONS: Access the Berlin Wall panels either from the Cobequid Trail along the river or from Dalhousie Agricultural Campus (from College Road, turn onto Farm Lane, then right onto Sipu Atwi, and left on Sheep Hill Lane). The panels are behind the agriculture buildings, just before you get to the trail, with a small footpath between them. Park on campus at various nearby lots (Haley Upper Parking Lot, Alumni Gardens parking lot, Rock Garden parking lot) but avoid reserved spaces.

MORE: Interestingly, there are two other places in Nova Scotia where you can see pieces of the Berlin Wall. Dartmouth's Peace Pavilion displays small fragments, and the town of Lunenburg boasts a panel that has had several homes over the years (at the time of writing, it was displayed in front of the Legion at 34 Duke Street).

26 Blue Beach: Canada's Birthplace of Vertebrate Paleontology

WHAT

A fossil-rich beach where the trackways of the first vertebrates to leave the sea and venture onto land 350 million years ago were found in 1841; the on-site museum features Atlantic Canada's largest collection of fossils.

WHERE

127 Blue Beach Road, Hantsport.

DETAILS

Our distant ancestors—and the ancestors of every mammal, amphibian, reptile, and bird to ever live on earth—took their first steps out of the sea onto land more than 350 million years ago. And some of these early steps, taken by four-legged prehistoric creatures called tetrapods, were recorded as fossilized footprints at Blue Beach.

These fossilized footprints, discovered in 1841, made Blue Beach the birthplace of vertebrate paleontology in Canada. Trackways from tetrapods during this time period are extremely rare, and this site is helping fill this gap in the global fossil record.

Today, the beach is still full of fossils, although the famous tetrapod trackways have been removed and displayed at the adjacent museum. It's difficult to walk on the beach and not see a fossil of some kind in the shale. In fact, in 2015, the jaw of a newly discovered species of ancient fish (*Sphyragnathus tyche*, a predatory, fanged species that would have been about a metre long) was discovered in Blue Beach's cliffs, currently the only known fossil of this species.

Less flashy but equally fascinating fossils also abound at Blue Beach. You may see ancient fossilized horsetail plants, which have survived the eons relatively unchanged to torment modern-day gardeners. Trace fossils that record the crawling or burrowing movement of creatures can also be found, along with impressions of waves and even raindrops, all preserved for millions of years in rock.

Before you venture down to the beach, stop at the museum by

the trailhead. It may look unassuming, but it contains the biggest collection of fossils in Atlantic Canada. You'll see fossilized plants from the earliest Carboniferous forests, over 2,000 rock slabs featuring fossilized footprints, remains of a gargantuan ancient fish that crawled on its fins, and the world's largest (and oldest) assortment of tetrapod fossils. Staff are available to guide you through the collections and help you identify what to look for on the beach.

ACCESSIBILITY: A rough trail and stairs lead down to the beach, so the beach itself is not wheelchair accessible. But the exhibit area in the museum is wheelchair accessible.

FEES: Museum (and beach) entry is free, but donations are accepted; open seasonally from May to October.

PARKING/DIRECTIONS: A small unpaved parking area serves both the museum and the beach. Several guided tours are available; check online for details.

MORE: A porta-potty is located just off the path to the beach.

Note that fossil collecting is illegal in Nova Scotia without a permit, but you can always take a photo of your finds, document the location, and share the information with the professionals at the museum. Visit bluebeachfossilmuseum.com for more information.

27 The Buried Ships of Summerville

WHAT

The beached remains of three 19th-century wooden sailing ships, one of which has a recently exposed hull.

WHERE

Hobart's Beach, Summerville (north of Windsor).

DETAILS

You never know what's lurking beneath the sand on Nova Scotia's beautiful beaches. Massive wooden sailing ships from the 1800s, for instance.

In the summer of 2024, flash flooding at Hobart's Beach in Summerville revealed the hull of a 60-metre-long, three-masted ship called the *Hamburg*, built on the Avon River in Hantsport and launched in the 1880s. The flooding washed away a section of the beach, leaving the side of the ship exposed, complete with wooden beams and wooden pegs. And the *Hamburg* is just one of three 19th-century sailing ships buried beneath the sand on the shores of the river.

Nova Scotia has a rich shipbuilding history, and this area enjoyed a reputation as a major shipbuilding and shipping centre during the 1800s. Ships were constructed, loaded with cargo, and travelled around the globe, returning with merchandise from faraway ports. The huge ships resting beneath the sands in Summerville once shipped lumber and gypsum overseas, until the invention of the steam engine rendered them obsolete.

All three ships were abandoned on Hobart's Beach a century ago

and, along with the now-buried wharf, caught fire in 1936. The remains were once much more visible than they are now—in fact, some older members of the community remember playing among the wrecks as children. Over time, as the extreme tides in the Bay of Fundy and Minas Basin raised and lowered the river daily by as much as 13 metres, the ships sank farther and farther into the red sands of Hobart's Beach, as gravel and silt filled in around them. At some point in the 1970s, they were completely buried, even at low tide.

By the time of the flash flooding 50 years later, many residents were completely unaware of the aging behemoths that lay silently beneath the beach. But now that a piece of that hidden maritime history has been revealed, it has rekindled local interest in the area's link to the Golden Age of Sail, intriguing visitors along the way.

ACCESSIBILITY: The beach is not wheelchair accessible; viewing the ship requires walking through mud, and any footwear not firmly attached will be quickly claimed by the beach.

FEES: None; can be visited year-round at low tide.

PARKING/DIRECTIONS: Hobart's Beach is at the end of Block Wharf Road. Follow the road until it ends at the pier and a free parking lot. Walk down the boat ramp and along the beach to the left until you see the ship. You'll also notice wooden remnants of the other two 19th-century ships emerging from the sand in various places.

MORE: Much of the beach is underwater at high tide, so the best time to see the *Hamburg*'s hull is at low tide; consult an online tide chart when planning your visit.

28 Burntcoat Head Park: Where the World's Highest Tides Come to Play

WHAT

A natural park where you can walk on the ocean floor and experience the world's highest tides.

WHERE

45 Faulkner Lane (formerly 627 Burntcoat Head Road), Noel.

DETAILS

There is no more dramatic place in the province to experience the remarkable tides of the Bay of Fundy than at Burntcoat Head Park.

This natural treasure boasts the title of "World's Highest Tides" (proclaimed in the *Guinness Book of World Records*). Arrive at low tide

to walk on the ocean floor and examine the tidal pools left by the receding waters, full of living sea creatures such as hermit crabs, mussels, and snails. A walk along the crimson shoreline reveals picturesque cliffs, rock formations, and caves of various sizes, temporarily accessible.

At high tide, the Bay of Fundy rushes in to raise the waterline by as much as 16 metres. The iconic resident flowerpot stack becomes an island, and the stairs carved into the rock are covered by water with impressive rapidity. The tide advances very quickly here, at a speed of 15 kilometres/hour, and staff ensure that visitors don't venture too close to the upper shelf of rock until the waters recede once more.

The difference between low and high tide is astonishing, and it's worth sticking around to see both. While you're waiting, you can experience another local natural phenomenon—a tidal bore. When the incoming tide meets a river flowing out to the ocean, it creates a tidal bore, or wave, temporarily reversing the flow of the river. Adventure seekers can even go tidal bore rafting in the Bay of Fundy to ride the waves themselves. Those just looking to see the tidal bore can visit a variety of spots along the bay, such as Dawson Dowel Park or the Fundy Tidal Interpretive Centre in South Maitland. For a full day of tides, arrive at Burntcoat Head Park at low tide, catch the tidal bore 3 hours later, and then return to Burntcoat for high tide 3 hours after that.

ACCESSIBILITY: Access to the ocean floor involves stairs and is not wheelchair accessible. The path around the park is made of mulch and crushed stone, with some elevation changes.

FEES: None to visit the site on your own. Guided tours are available for a cost. The gift shop and washrooms are open seasonally from May to October, but the site itself can be visited outside these hours, at your own risk.

PARKING/DIRECTIONS: Abundant free on-site parking.

MORE: Proper footwear is essential if you're walking on the ocean floor, which can be very slippery. You will get muddy (an on-site foot-wash station is available).

Try not to walk in tidal pools to avoid crushing fragile sea life. If you pick up any creatures, be sure to return them gently to their homes.

Check tide times online or on the sign posted on site, and return to safety in plenty of time to avoid being stranded by high tide and having to be rescued. Visit burntcoatheadpark.ca for more information.

29 Courthouse Hill:
Five Counties, One Look-off

WHAT

A memorial site and scenic viewpoint with panoramic views of the countryside, where it's possible to see five counties from one spot.

WHERE

Courthouse Hill Road, in East Gore, between Truro and Windsor.

DETAILS

Nestled amid rolling hills and surrounded by farmland as far as the eye can see is Courthouse Hill in central Hants County.

It's hard to believe that this bucolic landscape, about as far removed from urban life as it's possible to be, was once the site of the East Hants Courthouse, which opened its doors in 1867 to conduct the business of the East Hants Municipality and its council. It was a local landmark until it was destroyed in 1954 by a fire; it was never rebuilt. But instead of fading into obscurity like countless other historical landmarks across the country, a memorial was created in 1980 as part of a commemoration of the centennial of the incorporation of the Municipality of East Hants, reminding visitors of what once stood on the spot.

Today, the main attraction for most visitors is the panoramic views afforded by the 186-metre-tall hill and the unobstructed pastoral vistas beyond. On a clear day, it's possible to see five of Nova Scotia's counties from this spot (Kings, Cumberland, Colchester, Pictou, and Hants). An on-site monument marks the spot on which the courthouse stood, and marked stones on the ground contain footprints oriented toward each of the five counties.

ACCESSIBILITY: The look-off area around the monument isn't paved, but it is fairly flat and accessible. There is some uneven ground between the parking area and the site, however.

FEES: None; can be visited year-round.

PARKING/DIRECTIONS: Take Courthouse Hill Road to the top of the hill, and the monument is visible by the road, fenced off from the actively farmed fields. Park at the side of the road and be aware of any farming vehicles in the vicinity, as this area is a working farm.

MORE: The farmland around the monument belongs to Courthouse Hill Farm, a ninth-generation family farm that also offers outdoor farm activities, including mountain bike races, obstacle courses, and a corn maze. It's a surreal sight to visit this serene historic spot while farming activities carry on around it.

30 Debert Diefenbunker:
A Cold War Relic

WHAT

A decommissioned 64,000-square-foot Cold War fallout shelter in a small farming community in central Nova Scotia.

Note: At the time of writing in 2026, the site is undergoing major renovations and isn't yet open to the public, but you can still view the exterior and the grounds, which boast several World War II-era structures.

WHERE

47 Lockheed Crescent, Debert (15 minutes from Truro).

DETAILS

An abandoned nuclear blast shelter is hardly what you expect to find in a small farming community in central Nova Scotia.

The Debert bunker was one of seven bomb shelters (dubbed "Diefenbunkers" because they were commissioned by prime minister John Diefenbaker in 1959) built in Canada during the Cold War. The bunker's concrete walls are 1 metre thick, and it was built to withstand a 5-megaton nuclear blast. Inside, relics of the Cold War era include decontamination showers, a CBC radio studio, a ventilation system that could screen out radioactive, chemical, and biological particles, and a doomsday-movie-worthy NORAD map room for tracking nuclear fallout.

Debert Diefenbunker was constructed to function as regional military and government headquarters if a nuclear strike occurred. Stored inside the bunker's nearly 6,000 square metres would have been sufficient water and food to allow up to 350 people to survive for a month and a half. The guest list would have been exclusive—for example, the premier, lieutenant-governor, and military officials—to be sure of continuity of government in a disaster situation.

In 1997, the bunker was decommissioned, along with its counterparts across the country. Since then, it has changed owners and purposes several times. Following the end of its military use, it was open for public tours. Beginning in 2013, it was run as an entertainment complex for events such as laser tag, escape rooms (appropriately featuring doomsday scenarios), paintball, and movie nights. Current plans involve converting the Diefenbunker into all-inclusive, state-of-the-art luxury accommodations, slated to open in 2026.

ACCESSIBILITY: The area around the bunker is flat and may be navigated by most visitors.

FEES: None; the exterior and surrounding area can be visited year-round.

PARKING/DIRECTIONS: Free on-site parking.

MORE: Even though there's no public entry to Debert Diefenbunker as of 2026, it's worth walking the grounds to be transported to a completely different era. The bunker site was formerly Camp Debert, used as a final staging area for troops embarking from Halifax during World War II.

To learn more about the site's history, visit the Debert Military Museum, housed in former World War II barracks, at 35 Acadia Avenue, just down the road from the bunker.

31 The Improbable Balancing Rock of Long Island

WHAT

A 20-tonne vertical pillar of basalt suspended improbably on a narrow rock ledge above St. Mary's Bay.

WHERE

Highway 217, Tiverton, Long Island (about an hour from Digby, including a short ferry ride).

DETAILS

As far as miraculous quirks of nature go, Long Island's Balancing Rock is hard to beat. It's as if a bunch of giants once played a game of Jenga, and then just left the last piece balanced perilously on the edge of a cliff, forever poised on the brink of falling into the ocean.

Thirty feet tall and weighing more than 20 tonnes, Balancing Rock is a basalt pillar that was formed from lava flows hundreds of millions of years ago. The tides and wind during that time have sculpted it into its current remarkable shape and gravity-defying position. Rumour has it that many years ago local fishermen tried to pull the imposing rock down with ropes, from their fishing boats. Their failure to do so is evidence that Balancing Rock is not as precariously balanced as it appears.

Access to this geological marvel is down a forest trail of approximately 2.5 kilometres, round trip. The hike is pleasant, but steep, consisting of a series of boardwalks and 253 stairs culminating in your arrival at the viewing platform directly across from the rock. The hike takes between 30 and 60 minutes, depending on how many photos you take (and how many times you rest on the way up all those stairs).

Interpretive panels describe local flora, fauna, and geology, and the views of St. Mary's Bay are jaw-dropping. Birdwatchers will be in their glory here, as will anyone lucky enough to view the seals that frequent the area.

ACCESSIBILITY: Given the hike and 253 steps, this site isn't wheelchair accessible. For those who wish to tackle the walk, there are benches where you can rest along the way.

FEES: None; the trail is technically open year-round but is maintained only from May to October.

PARKING/DIRECTIONS: Balancing Rock is located near Tiverton on Long Island, accessible via the Petit Passage Ferry from East Ferry (Digby Neck). The ferry is free and leaves the mainland on the half hour, returning to East Ferry from Tiverton on the hour. The free parking area for Balancing Rock is well marked and just a few minutes from the ferry at Tiverton.

MORE: Sturdy footwear is advisable for the hike to Balancing Rock.

You can also catch a ferry from Freeport, Long Island, if you want to explore adjacent Brier Island.

32 Interactive Mi'kmaw Experiences:
Millbrook Cultural and Heritage Centre

WHAT

An Indigenous-run facility offering a multi-sensory, interactive experience with Mi'kmaw history and culture, including music, Mi'kmaw language, arts and crafts, ancient artifacts, and cultural interpreters.

WHERE

65 Treaty Trail, Millbrook (just outside Truro).

DETAILS

There's nowhere better for visitors of all ages to celebrate and learn about Mi'kmaw culture than the Millbrook Cultural & Heritage Centre.

For thousands of years before Europeans set foot in Nova Scotia, the Mi'kmaq thrived here, calling their territory "Mi'kma'ki." They had a reciprocal relationship with the land, subsisting on fishing and hunting, and travelled seasonally between small interior camps in the winter and larger camps along the coast in the summer. Later, they traded with Europeans and enjoyed close relationships with the French and the Acadians, with whom they fought to resist the British takeover of the region.

The treaties signed in the 1700s between the Mi'kmaq and the British Crown were a commitment to peace and coexistence, but the Mi'kmaq never surrendered any land to the British, which means the entire province of Nova Scotia exists within Mi'kmaw unceded territory. A visit to the Millbrook Cultural & Heritage Centre is an accessible, interactive way to get a fascinating glimpse of the lives, culture, and history of the Mi'kmaq, whether you are a visitor to, or a resident of, Mi'kma'ki.

Wig-wom
WIGWAM
Please Remove Shoes
Before Entering The
Wigwam ☺

PLEASE DO NOT TOUCH THE ANIMALS
PLEASE DO NOT TOUCH THE ANIMALS

You'll be greeted by a full-size wigwam that you're welcome to enter (remove your footwear first). Examples of animals important to Mi'kmaw culture are displayed, along with their Mi'kmaw names, including pronunciation. In fact, all exhibits in the centre are bilingual, underscoring the vital role language plays in the identity of the Mi'kmaq and reflecting the resurgence of interest in Mi'kmaw language, which has survived despite attempts to stamp it out in the former Shubenacadie Indian Residential School.

Visitors can learn the Mi'kmaw alphabet, listen to examples of Mi'kmaw words and then practice them. There's a collection of arrowheads, hand axes, and other artifacts dating back almost 8,000 years, examples of Mi'kmaw beadwork, woven baskets, and even a birchbark canoe. Other treasures include an intricate example of ceremonial Mi'kmaw attire from the 1800s, recently repatriated from Australia, and a rock bearing Mi'kmaw petroglyphs moved from Red Bridge Pond in Dartmouth.

In addition to displays with information on Mi'kmaw history and culture, you can get hands-on by touching porcupine quills and furs, smelling sweetgrass, and listening to Mi'kmaw music. Interpreters are eager to share stories, answer questions, and conduct tours of the centre to enrich your visit. Don't miss the 12-metre-tall statue of Glooscap in the back courtyard. Glooscap, a legendary hero representing wisdom and hope, who figures prominently in Mi'kmaw creation stories, remains culturally significant to the Mi'kmaq today.

To learn more about Mi'kmaw culture and history, visit Kejimkujik National Park and National Historic Site, where cultural programs like petroglyph tours and birchbark canoe building are offered, and the site of the former/demolished Shubenacadie Indian Residential School, now a National Historic Site.

ACCESSIBILITY: The Millbrook Cultural & Heritage Centre is fully wheelchair accessible.

FEES: Admission is charged (entry for all Millbrook Band Members is free upon presentation of a band card); there's an additional small fee for an interpreter-guided tour. Adults: $7 / Seniors (65+): $4 / Child (6–17): $4.50 / Child under 5: free. Family (2 Adults and Children under 18): $18 / Adult Tours: $5/person

PARKING/DIRECTIONS: Free on-site parking.

MORE: The centre also offers workshops—some involving additional costs—including drum making, journey stones, talking sticks, and the traditional Mi'kmaw game of waltes (a game of chance played with six disc-shaped dice).

The gift shop sells one-of-a-kind items from Mi'kmaw artisans and Mi'kmaw businesses and an extensive selection of books for adults and children. Free tea and coffee are offered in the lobby. Visit millbrookheritagecentre.ca for more information.

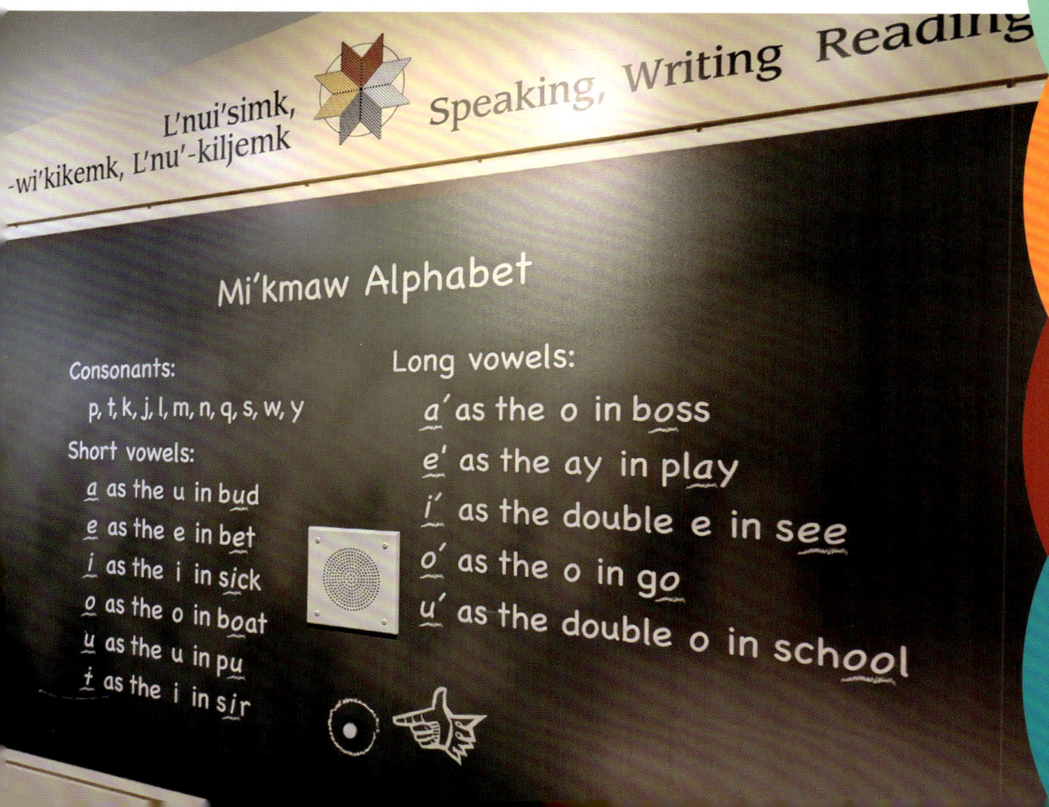

33 Maud Lewis Memorial Park: An Ode to Canada's Beloved Folk Artist

WHAT

A memorial for beloved Canadian folk artist Maud Lewis, on the site of the original tiny home and studio where she created her cheerful, whimsical artwork.

WHERE

511 Highway 1 Marshalltown, Maud Lewis Lane, a few minutes west of Digby in Marshalltown.

DETAILS

Generations of admirers have been entranced by Canadian folk artist Maud Lewis's whimsical paintings, with their brightly coloured, cheerful scenes of rural life in Nova Scotia. Few, however, have visited the site where she lived and painted her joyful works of art.

Lewis's instantly recognizable paintings feature charming, childlike depictions of wide-eyed cats, multi-hued tulips, and idyllic scenes of life in the Maritimes. But the artist's own life was far from idyllic. She was plagued with physical birth defects and rheumatoid arthritis that worsened throughout her life, eventually rendering her barely able to hold a paintbrush. Yet she found joy and comfort in her art from a young age.

Lewis painted and sold her own Christmas cards as a child, and she would later sell her paintings out of her house for as little as $2 or $3, initially to passersby. Once her fame grew, she and her artwork became a tourist attraction. She even sold several paintings to the president of the United States, but reportedly she never sold any piece during her lifetime for more than $10. Today, Lewis's paintings have been known to fetch hundreds of thousands of dollars.

For over 30 years, Lewis lived with her husband in a tiny house measuring no more than 170 square feet in Marshalltown, just outside Digby. The couple lived in poverty, and their small home lacked running water and electricity. One thing it didn't lack was character: Lewis covered their home with her delightful artwork. Walls, warming oven, furniture, breadbox—every available surface was fair game for Lewis's vibrantly painted flowers, birds, and butterflies.

This memorial sits on the exact spot of the tiny house where Lewis lived and created her enduring artwork, and it's also the same shape and size as the original home. Designed by architect Brian MacKay-Lyons, the severe steel replica and its primary-coloured accents are meant to symbolize the contrast between the harsh reality of Lewis's life and the whimsical lens through which she viewed the world. On-site interpretive panels tell the story of Maud's life and art and provide information on her original home and the memorial itself.

Lewis's original house was saved from dilapidation in 1979, when it was sold to the Art Gallery of Nova Scotia. Disassembled and lovingly restored, the home, complete with Lewis's artwork inside and out, is now on permanent display at the AGNS.

ACCESSIBILITY: The site is on flat ground and is wheelchair accessible.

FEES: None; can be visited year-round.

PARKING/DIRECTIONS: Free on-site parking. While the official address for the memorial is 511 Highway 1, Marshalltown, you may have more luck searching for Maud Lewis Lane, which is the closest side street. The site is well marked by a large sign.

MORE: Visit the memorial anytime—there's no entry into the structure, but you can peek through the metal slats to glimpse the spartan interior. There's also a garden, picnic table, and benches on site.

34 Medford Beach Sandstone Stacks

WHAT

Other-worldly sandstone formations rising above the Bay of Fundy, accessible by foot at low tide or by kayak at high tide.

WHERE

Canning, Kings County, a 20-minute drive north of Wolfville (accessible via Kingsport Beach, NS-221, Canning).

DETAILS

Like all the best discoveries, a trip to the sandstone stacks at Medford Beach is as much about the journey as the destination. As direct access can be gained only by trespassing in a farmer's field, take the scenic route instead. The 4-kilometre journey (each way) easily takes 2.5 to 3 hours round-trip, depending on your comfort level on muddy terrain (and the amount of time you stop to take photos, which could be extensive, given the beauty of the shoreline). There's no marked trail, as the route is completely covered by the ocean at high tide.

Along the way, sandstone cliffs rise around you, the sedimentary rock taking fantastical shapes thanks to ongoing erosion by the Minas Basin's 12-metre tides. At low tide, vast red sand and mud flats are revealed, and the landscape looks like a slice of Mars transplanted to Nova Scotia. Numerous caves appear when the tide goes out, and sea creatures take refuge in the many tidal pools on the ocean floor. There's an excellent chance of spotting an eagle, along with seabirds, sea life, and whatever flotsam and jetsam has washed up onshore.

Medford Beach looks a little different today than it did in the recent past. In 2020, two of the keyhole arches collapsed from especially strong tides, a harsh reminder of the effects of climate change. The remaining sandstone formations are still worth the effort to visit them—and you'll likely have the trail and your destination to yourself. Visit in a kayak at high tide to see Medford Beach in a whole new way.

ACCESSIBILITY: The trek to the stacks is not wheelchair accessible and involves a difficult and muddy walk.

FEES: None.

PARKING/DIRECTIONS: Park at Kingsport Beach, at the juncture of NS-221 and Water Street in Canning. Walk left along the beach, and follow the coast for 4 kilometres until you see the sandstone stacks.

MORE: Cottages close to the stacks can be rented, with stairs down to the shore, for those who want to avoid the 4-kilometre hike.

Check the tide times online before setting out, to make sure that you don't get stranded. Starting the hike a few hours before low tide will give you sufficient time to return before the tide does.

You will get muddy, so proper footwear is important—if your shoes aren't properly secured, you will end up battling the mud for possession of them. It's a good idea to bring a change of footwear, as well as lots of water and sun protection, as there's no shade along the route.

35 Nova Scotia's Concrete House and Fairy Cottages

WHAT

The concrete house and whimsical fairy cottages created by visionary Charles Macdonald.

WHERE

Concrete House: 19 Saxon Street, Centreville.
Fairy Cottages: Huntington Point, near Halls Harbour.

DETAILS

It's been called the most unique home in Nova Scotia, and for good reason: the house at 19 Saxon Street in Centreville was sculpted entirely out of concrete, inside and out.

Built in 1910 by artist, sailor, environmentalist, socialist, and passionate concrete manufacturer Charles Macdonald, the structure was originally a cement brick factory. At the time, Macdonald was mocked by locals who didn't see the potential in what was then an uncommon material. That changed with World War I and the demand for concrete. After Macdonald married in 1915, he and his wife converted the former factory into their home, complete with concrete bathtub, fireplace, fences, and whimsical garden sculptures. The house has been little altered since, and the house and grounds, listed together on the Canadian Register of Historic Places, are currently operated as a museum.

While he was influenced by the architecture that he saw in his travels to Italy, the Caribbean, India, and beyond, Macdonald's artistic touch is evident everywhere—look for the handprints set into a concrete windowsill. His paintings are on display inside his home,

and a walk through the enchanting statue garden and one-of-a-kind house provides a charming glimpse into the life and artistic mind of a legendary Nova Scotian.

A mere 15 minutes away, tucked along a quiet gravel road that ends at the Bay of Fundy, are four other examples of Macdonald's artistry: the "faerie cottages" he had built in the 1930s to create income for his staff (and as a canvas for his artistic vision) during the Great Depression. Five cottages were originally built at Huntington Point, where the artist and his wife often enjoyed camping. Fashioned from concrete and stone and reinforced with driftwood and iron, each cottage was uniquely shaped, asymmetrical, and painted in bright colours.

Today, only four of the original five cottages remain, and, while they're not open to the public, they're well worth looking at from the outside. Three are private residences, while the Blue Cottage is owned by the Charles Macdonald House of Centreville Society and rented out each summer. If you become a paid member of the society and pay the fixed donation, you may stay at this heritage property for a week.

ACCESSIBILITY: The first floor of Concrete House is barrier-free, but there is a small threshold to get in, and the door is not quite 36 inches wide. Visitors with physical limitations can park in front of the garage door rather than in the parking lot, allowing them access onto the cement patio.

FEES: None, although donations are accepted. Concrete House is open for self-guided tours from June to August.

PARKING/DIRECTIONS: Free on-site parking for Concrete House, and you'll easily find it using the address provided above. The fairy cottages are not as easy to find, however. Head south past Halls Harbour and take the first road on the right (Simpson Road); turn right on Huntington Point Road, which ends at the beach. The cottages are scattered along the road. Parking is minimal—there's a tiny gravel parking lot at the beach.

MORE: Visit concretehouse.ca for more information.

36 The "Old Barn" on Stannus Street:
Canada's Oldest Indoor Hockey Rink

WHAT

The oldest indoor hockey rink in Canada, possibly North America, in the town that is a contender for the title of "Birthplace of Hockey."

WHERE

At Stannus Street and Thomas Street in Windsor, beside the Hants Aquatic Centre.

Note: While the town of Windsor considered purchasing the building in 2016, as of 2026 it remains in private hands and isn't open to the public—but even viewing it from the outside is a treat for hockey fans.

DETAILS

Windsor, Nova Scotia, has long claimed to be the "Birthplace of Hockey," a designation recognized and celebrated by the Windsor Hockey Heritage Society. It's not the only Canadian city to have made such a claim, and a game similar to hockey was played by the Mi'kmaq long before European contact. But while the origins of hockey may be contentious, one thing is for certain: the oldest indoor hockey rink in Canada—if not North America—can be found right here.

The Stannus Street Rink was built in 1897, before large-scale refrigeration was available. This "old barn"—a term of endearment for old arenas like this one—was for many years the only game in town when it came to sports venues, and it drew large crowds. Every winter, an ice rink was created inside the arena, but without refrigeration, the rink depended on Nova Scotia's fickle weather conditions. Locals would look to the flagpole on top of the building's steeple to find out if the ice was ready. A flying flag meant that hockey was on; no flag meant that the rink was too slushy, and no game could be played that night.

Throughout the 20th century, the Stannus Street Rink was home to two hockey teams, and it also hosted community and company teams. From 1905 to 1916, the Windsor Swastikas played their home games here. Their name was chosen before Nazi Germany forever altered the world's perception of the ancient symbol associated with prosperity and good luck; the team disbanded during World War I. The rink later became home to the Windsor Maple Leafs, a senior amateur hockey team that played in the Valley Senior Hockey League and later the Nova Scotia Senior Hockey League. The 1963–1964 Windsor Maple Leafs team was even inducted into the Nova Scotia Sports Hall of Fame.

Once the Hants Exhibition Arena was built in the 1960s, the Stannus Street Rink stopped being used as a hockey venue. Nowadays, it's used as winter storage for boats, motorcycles, RVs, and other vehicles. While it no longer hosts hockey games, the old barn on Stannus Street still has its share of fans. The Windsor Hockey Heritage Society would like to see the rink turned into a hockey museum to ensure that it is preserved and enjoyed by future generations, but no plans have been made yet.

ACCESSIBILITY: The gravel lot and grass surrounding the rink are flat and may be suitable for many visitors with physical limitations.

FEES: None (currently no public access to the interior).

PARKING/DIRECTIONS: Free parking in the gravel lot in front of the rink.

MORE: Hockey fans may also want to visit Windsor's Birthplace of Hockey Museum, which occupies a wing of the Clifton Museum. Long Pond, purportedly the "Cradle of Hockey," where early hockey games were played in Windsor as far back as 1800, may also be of interest.

The NS Textiles, one of many community/company hockey teams that played at Stannus Street Rink, 1935.

SPACE FOR RENT
Winter Storage For
RV's / Motorcycles / Boats
Cars & Trucks
DEBBY

37 Sinclair House's Mysterious Painted Room

WHAT

A mysterious painted room, possibly painted by early Masons, hidden within a 300-year-old national treasure.

WHERE

Second Floor, Sinclair Inn Museum, 230 St. George Street, Annapolis Royal.

DETAILS

A 300-year-old house can hold secrets within its walls—and, as it turns out, on them, too.

The history of the building known today as the Sinclair Inn Museum dates to at least 1710, and it holds quite a few honours. It's the oldest surviving Acadian structure in the country, it is Canada's second-oldest wooden building (the oldest is the deGannes house, a private residence also located in Annapolis Royal), and it's a National Historic Site. Sinclair Inn served many functions throughout its three centuries, from tavern to Masonic Lodge to taxi business. The house is now owned by the Annapolis Heritage Society.

In the 1960s, a leaking roof led to water damage in a second-floor room, prompting the discovery of painted images behind dozens of layers of wallpaper. Decades later, in 2016, the job of removing the layers of wallpaper began, with the assistance of an art conservator. The work revealed wall-to-wall, floor-to-ceiling, intricately painted murals. No one's completely sure of the age of the murals (although the best guess is the 1840s), who painted them, or why. But experts

believe they hail from the British period of the house's history, rather than French, when this Acadian treasure was built.

The murals depict a panoramic landscape scene featuring mountains, a lake, a house, and a waterfall—perhaps the mystery painter was inspired by the landscape? Masonic imagery such as a Greco-Roman column and arch suggests that early Masons may have been involved in the paintings (the first Masonic meetings in Canada were held in this building). The paintings are reminiscent of continental European frescoes, suggesting that maybe the painter(s) had travelled in Europe. The addition of a train to a wall by a less-practiced, more childlike hand also supports

SINCLAIR INN
MUSEUM
NATIONAL
HISTORIC
SITE
SINCLAIR
INN

this notion, as no one living in the area would have seen a train when the mural was created.

There are places where multiple images have been revealed, layered on top of one another, such as the faint impression of large ferns and vines visible over a large section of wall. These hint that the murals may have been added to by different people at different times. The wall's biggest mystery is the portrait of an officer, containing a combination of uniform details found during the 1700s and 1800s. Some have drawn a link between the painting and Prince Albert, consort to Queen Victoria, but the officer's identity remains a mystery to this day.

ACCESSIBILITY: Sinclair House is not wheelchair accessible and features narrow stairs and uneven floors.

FEES: Admission is by donation; the museum is open seasonally, from May through October.

PARKING/DIRECTIONS: No on-site parking; use nearby street parking.

MORE: The painted room is open only when the museum has two staff members available to lead tours. Before you visit, contact staff, and they will do their best to have the room open for you. Visit annapolisheritagesociety.com/sinclair-inn-museum for more information.

38 Stewiacke's Halfway Marker between the Equator and the North Pole

WHAT

A marker representing the exact halfway point between the equator and the North Pole, at the culmination of a dead-end lane in rural Stewiacke; it feels a world away from the nearby spectacle of Mastodon Ridge that celebrates the halfway point.

WHERE

Landmark Lane, off Riverside Road, just outside Stewiacke.

DETAILS

For motorists on Highway 102, signs at Exit 11 proclaiming Stewiacke (and its main tourist draw, Mastodon Ridge) to be halfway between the North Pole and the equator are a familiar sight. But the exact location of the actual Halfway Marker might surprise you.

The town of Stewiacke is known for its location halfway between the equator and the North Pole. There's even an official stamp from 1995 declaring the town's position. Stewiacke's Mastodon Ridge has long celebrated the town's coordinates and is a popular spot featuring a visitor centre, mini-golf, a playground, fast food restaurants, ice cream shop, and a life-size mastodon replica.

However, sticklers for accuracy and seekers of the unusual will appreciate knowing that the exact location of the halfway point is actually not at Mastodon Ridge at all—though staff are happy to point you in the right direction. The official, exact marker location is mentioned on one of the informative panels on site at Mastodon Ridge.

Just don't expect the pomp and circumstance of Mastodon Ridge here: the only indication that you're not trespassing in someone's backyard is a simple sign informing that "you are now exactly halfway between the Equator and the North Pole."

ACCESSIBILITY: Although the ground around the site is comprised of grass and gravel, it is relatively flat. The sign can also be easily be seen from a vehicle.

FEES: None; can be visited year-round.

PARKING/DIRECTIONS: To find the Halfway Marker, drive 2 kilometres from Mastodon Ridge, across the Stewiacke River to Landmark Lane. The marker is on the right-hand side of a dead-end roadway, where it's been since 1938, when a survey crew working for the Government of Canada determined the precise spot.

There is no formal parking lot, but since you likely won't meet a soul, you won't need one—simply pull off to the side of the road. If you are walking or cycling, access the spot via the Stewiacke River Trail via Mastodon Ridge.

MORE: Geography buffs may wonder why the marker is not located at the 45th parallel north (that is, it's not at exactly 45 degrees latitude). In fact, because the earth is not a perfect sphere—it is flatter at the poles, and bulges at the equator—the precise halfway mark is slightly greater than 45 degrees, placing it right here at 45°08'40".

Wondering about the mastodon connection to Mastodon Ridge? For thousands of years, mastodons roamed what is now Nova Scotia, and their remains have been found across the province. Mastodon Ridge is named for one such find at a nearby quarry. You can hike Mastodon Trail, which starts behind Carroll's Corner Community Centre near Milford, for a glimpse of the gypsum mine where mastodon bones were discovered.

YOU ARE NOW EXACTLY
HALFWAY BETWEEN
THE EQUATOR AND
THE NORTH POLE

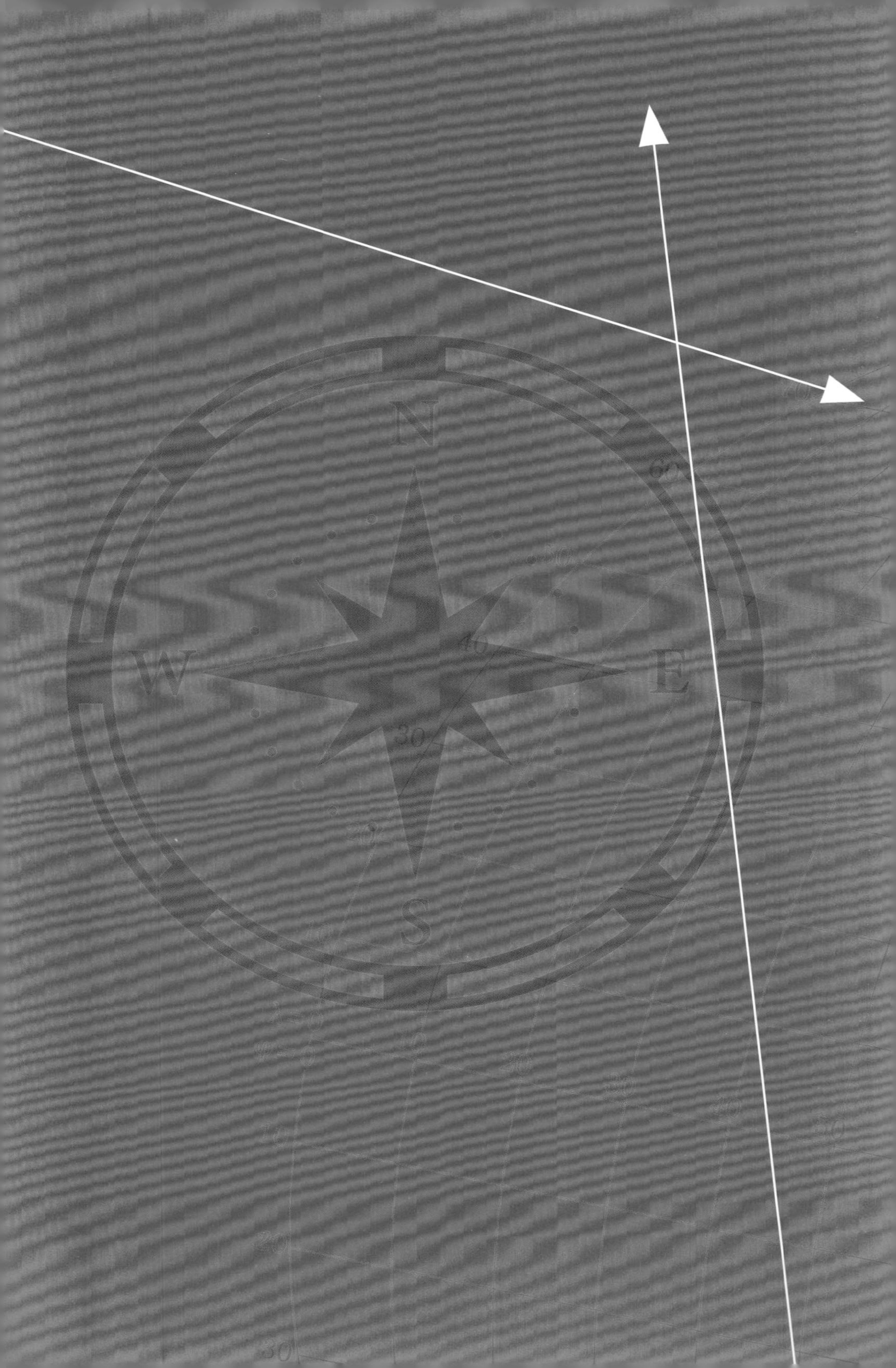
N
W
E
S

NØRTHUMBERLAND SHORE

The warmest ocean water in the province beckons along the Northumberland Shore's hundreds of kilometres of beaches. This region is the gateway to both New Brunswick and Prince Edward Island, and it's where the first Scottish settlers in Nova Scotia landed and established a permanent settlement.

39 The Clown Grave of Pictou

WHAT

The clown-topped grave of acrobat, clown, and beloved local icon George "Twitter" William Johnston.

WHERE

Haliburton Cemetery, 8104 Sunrise Trail, Pictou.

DETAILS

As far as unusual tombstones go, a grave adorned with a clown is tough to beat. What's the story behind the Pictou man memorialized by this whimsical, yet tragic, grave marker?

George William Johnston, known to locals and audiences by his clown name "Twitter," was born on March 29, 1889, and wore many hats in his 73 years. A trained acrobat, Twitter worked as trapeze artist, tumbler, pantomime performer, machinist, clown, CBC Radio performer, and sleight-of-hand artist, touring the US and the Maritimes extensively as he performed. During World War II, Twitter put on war bonds benefit shows to raise money for the war effort.

Twitter loved entertaining and was a local legend in his home of Pictou; the mention of his name would elicit smiles and fond stories, and he was in the midst of telling his autobiography to a broadcaster and columnist when he died. Despite his diminutive size at 5 feet 2 inches tall, he had a big heart, and his kindness was as legendary as his performing skills.

The unusual grave has garnered its share of attention, along with a reputation for spooky activity. A variety of paranormal activity has been reported here—eerie feelings, mysterious lights and sounds,

TWITTER
GEORGE WILLIAM JOHNSTON
1889 — 1962
MCKEAN
JOHNSTON

disembodied voices, and objects that are left in one place and move when someone turns away. It's been said that the clown's eyes follow visitors as they walk around the cemetery and that its hand is sometimes in a different position upon a second glance at the gravesite. One thing is certain, however: George "Twitter" Johnston was the heart of his community and lived to entertain all who knew him.

ACCESSIBILITY: The cemetery has gravel pathways and well-tended lawns.

FEES: None; can be visited year-round.

PARKING/DIRECTIONS: The Haliburton Cemetery is clearly marked. Follow the loop counterclockwise until you get to the end of the cemetery and have started driving back toward the entrance. The grave is on your right as you drive back to the entrance; park at the side of the gravel path.

MORE: Please do not leave donations of money at the grave, as the plexiglass protecting the clown has previously been broken by vandals to get at the coins left by visitors.

40 The *Hector*: A Piece of Living History

WHAT

A painstakingly restored replica of the three-masted ship that brought the first Scottish settlers to Nova Scotia in 1773.

WHERE

33 Caladh Avenue, Pictou waterfront.

DETAILS

In 1773, 189 people left Scotland for Nova Scotia on the *Hector*, lured by promises of fertile farmland, food provisions, and prosperity in the British colonies. At *Hector* Heritage Quay in Pictou, you can board a full-size replica of the ship that brought them here.

Life aboard the crowded, outdated Dutch cargo ship *Hector* was dismal and worsened by the fact that a hurricane extended the journey from six to 11 weeks. Quarters were extremely cramped and unsanitary, and passengers competed with rats for scraps of food, battling seasickness and illness in the hope of making a better life for themselves and their families in the New World.

The *Hector*'s passengers were devastated when they finally arrived in Pictou and saw the land that they had been promised, which turned out not to be cleared farmland but heavily forested land that they didn't have the skills or tools to clear. When the settlers refused their lots, they were in turn denied their promised food provisions—all with winter quickly approaching. The local Mi'kmaq were key to the settlers' survival, teaching them how to hunt, ice fish, and make and use snowshoes. Without this assistance, the settlers wouldn't have survived

AS
STAR
CONSTANT AS THE NORTHERN
HECTOR
PICTOU N.S.

the winter. In time, they learned to clear trees and built farmsteads throughout Pictou County and beyond, establishing the first enduring Scottish community in the province and earning Pictou the title of "the Birthplace of New Scotland."

In the 1990s, a full-sized replica of the three-masted ship was built using the original plans, but by 2020 it had deteriorated and was removed from the water for repairs. During the next five years, master shipbuilders and craftspeople worked to restore the ship, finally launching it back into the water in July 2025.

Visitors can now board the *Hector* and experience what life would have been like for the 189 people who spent nearly three months in its confines. Work on the ship continues as the ambitious multi-year restoration project progresses, with the goal of having a completed, operational ship with full rigging ready for tours in Pictou harbour by the summer of 2027.

Explore the Interpretive Centre at *Hector* Heritage Quay for an introduction to the ship and the history it represents, before boarding the *Hector* to step back in time.

ACCESSIBILITY: The Interpretive Centre is wheelchair accessible. As of 2026, the *Hector* itself has a ramp for entry onto the main deck; however, access to the below-deck display is via wooden ladders.

FEES: Admission is charged to enter the Interpretive Centre, but at the time of writing there was no fee to enter the ship itself, although donations are accepted. Both are open seasonally, from June to October.

Admission for the Interpretive Centre: Adults: $10 / Seniors: $8 / Children under 15: free / Families: $24

PARKING/DIRECTIONS: Free on-site museum parking at the *Hector* Heritage Quay, and free street parking nearby.

MORE: Visit shiphectorcampaign.com for more information.

41 Thinkers Lodge:
The Birthplace of Peace

WHAT

The historic house where the nuclear disarmament movement began; it's also the only place outside Ottawa where you can see one of Canada's two Nobel Peace Prizes.

WHERE

249 Water Street, Pugwash.

DETAILS

It's known as the "birthplace of peace," but many remain unaware of the existence of Thinkers Lodge—or its incredible and ongoing significance to global peace.

Perched on an isolated, beautifully landscaped spot along the Northumberland Strait in the tiny village of Pugwash, this sprawling home was built over 200 years ago. But its legacy stems from a much more recent historic event: the world's first nuclear disarmament peace talks, held here in 1957.

At the height of the Cold War, the Russell-Einstein Manifesto, released in 1955, drew attention to the dangers of nuclear weapons and called for scientists around the world to convene to assess these dangers and work toward resolving them peacefully. In response, a conference was planned where scientists could do exactly that. Cyrus Eaton, a businessman and philanthropist, offered to host the conference at his "Thinkers Lodge" in Pugwash.

In July 1957, 22 world-renowned scientists hailing from both sides of the Iron Curtain assembled for the first Pugwash Conference on

Joined by Antoine Lacassagne, Cyrus Eaton, and Dmitri Skobeltzyn, Joseph Rotblat issued a statement to the press on the great success of the Pugwash Conference at Thinkers Lodge, 1957.

Science and World Affairs, a groundbreaking meeting that launched a movement to advocate for nuclear disarmament and world peace. Along with plenary sessions, the conference included informal elements such as croquet on the expansive grounds and meals together in the dining hall, where scientists exchanged ideas and solidified their commitment to peace. The Pugwash Conferences continue to bring public figures and scientists together for gatherings across the globe so that they can work toward disarmament and peace.

Thinkers Lodge is a National Historic Site and a symbol of scientific collaboration, diplomacy, and peace. Today, conferences, retreats, workshops, weddings, and other gatherings are held on this serene, historic spot. The lodge also functions as a museum, with informative panels describing the Pugwash Conferences and its key players. On display, notably, is the Nobel Peace Prize awarded jointly to the Pugwash Conferences and to key founder/organizer Joseph Rotblat, whose wish it was for the medal to remain at the birthplace of peace.

ACCESSIBILITY: The main floor of Thinkers Lodge is fully wheelchair accessible. Upstairs bedrooms require the ability to navigate stairs, but all the information and displays are located on the main floor.

FEES: None; open seasonally from June to August for free self-guided and guided tours. In September and October, tours are offered by appointment only; contact staff in advance of your visit.

PARKING/DIRECTIONS: Free on-site parking is available.

MORE: Visit thinkerslodge.org for more information.

42 Train Station Inn and Railway Dining Car

WHAT

A 19th-century train station and vintage Canadian boxcars and cabooses converted into accommodations, restaurant, and gift shop.

WHERE

21 Station Road, Tatamagouche.

DETAILS

Train Station Inn in Tatamagouche offers what might be the most unusual dining and accommodation experience in Nova Scotia.

Built around 1887, the Tatamagouche Station serviced the Intercolonial Railway's "Short Line" from Oxford Junction to Stellerton (later taken over by Canadian National Railway) until it stopped welcoming passengers in 1960. By 1973, the building was scheduled to be demolished—until a local high school student and train lover bought the station. The station has since been converted into an eclectic gift shop and a café featuring locally roasted coffee.

But the vintage Canadian train cars are the attraction. They line the train tracks behind the shop and café, as if they've just pulled into the station. These boxcars and cabooses are the real deal, with the oldest dating back more than a century. While on the outside they might look like they've rolled in from the 19th century, inside they've been redesigned to function as modern suites, with all the comforts of home. The spacious suites each feature a private bathroom, and depending on the train car, you may find a kitchenette, private deck, seating areas, bathtub, multiple beds, and even original conductor seats in a caboose cupola.

You can drop by the 1928 railway dining car for a bite to eat even if you're not staying in this boutique hotel. Reservations are recommended, but walk-ins can often be accommodated. The menu features dishes made from local produce, served out of a vintage CN Railway train car that once transported soldiers and newcomers from Halifax's Pier 21 to points across the country. Live music nights on the platform feature music and bar service under the stars.

ACCESSIBILITY: A ramp leads into the train station building, where you'll find the gift shop, café, and accessible washrooms. However, steps must be navigated to access the train cars themselves. An accessible outdoor kitchen with a limited menu and live music is open Mondays, Wednesdays, and Fridays.

FEES: None to enter; the dining car, rooms, gift shop, and café are all open seasonally from May to October; check online for details.

PARKING/DIRECTIONS: Free on-site parking.

MORE: Don't miss the swanky train car outfitted as a drawing room, connected to the dining car (past the washrooms). Visit tatatrainstation.com for more information.

RAILWAY
DINING

AR
CANADIAN
NATIONAL
CB&CNS

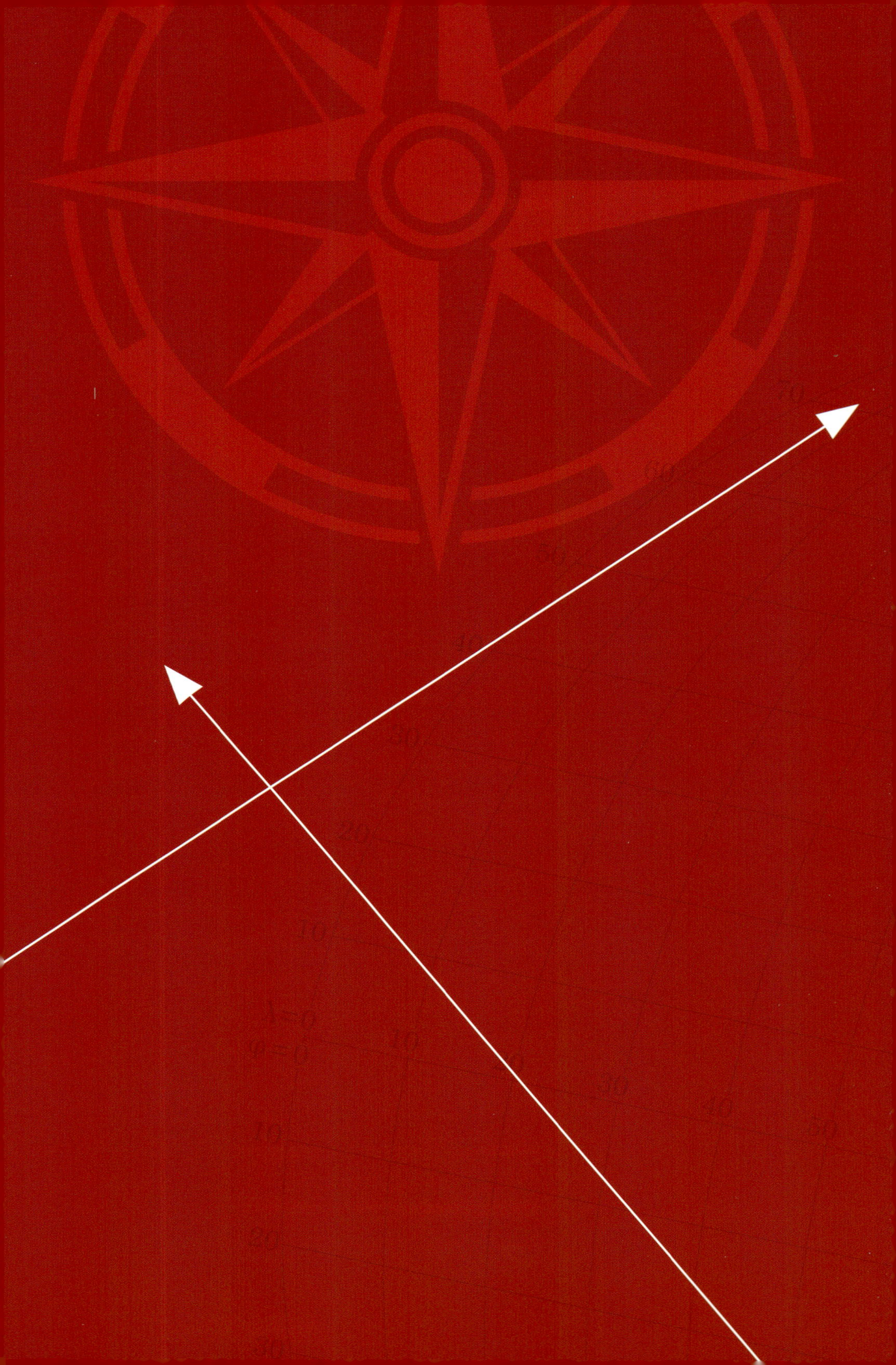

CAPE BRETØN ISLAND

The island of Cape Breton boasts some of the most jaw-dropping scenery in the province. Drive or hike along the famed Cabot Trail, go whale watching, and celebrate Gaelic culture by joining a céilidh for an evening of Gaelic music and dance. And carve out some time for the quirky hidden gems the island has to offer.

43 Broughton:
Cape Breton's Ghost Town

WHAT

A long-abandoned mining town now reclaimed by wilderness, also believed to have been the site of the first revolving door in North America.

WHERE

Broughton, Cape Breton (about half an hour from Sydney).

DETAILS

One of Canada's first planned towns, designed to house over 10,000 people, now lies in ruins in the backwoods of Cape Breton, a forgotten shadow of its former splendour.

The discovery of coal at the turn of the 20th century spurred the formation of the Cape Breton Coal, Iron, and Railway Company. It was run by a pair of Englishmen with an ambitious plan: to raise millions of dollars and turn the former farming community of Broughton into a state-of-the-art town with all the modern conveniences of the day. With wide boulevards inspired by New York City and a Halifax architect spearheading the design of its Gothic Revival buildings, the town featured two huge hotels, dozens of miners' houses, several stores and churches, offices, and a school. The Broughton Arms Hotel was the town's crown jewel, rumoured to be the best hotel this side of Montreal—it's even credited with having the first revolving door on the continent.

At its height in 1906, Broughton housed around 1,000 residents. But a combination of isolation, competition from coal and rail companies, transportation problems, and a shortage of investors spelled disaster for the burgeoning town, and by 1907, the Cape Breton Coal, Iron, and Railroad Company was bankrupt.

During World War I, more than 1,200 soldiers from the 185th Cape Breton Highlanders were trained and housed in the town, but after that, it was largely abandoned; the encroaching forest has now wholly reclaimed Broughton. In fact, driving along Broughton Road today, you'd have no idea that a town constructed for tens of thousands of people once existed here. But intrepid adventurers who don't mind searching will quickly find remnants of this abandoned town lurking in the overgrown foliage. The vast foundations of both Broughton hotels can be explored, along with a forgotten cemetery and the ruins of dozens of miner homes and other buildings.

ACCESSIBILITY: Broughton is not wheelchair accessible and features rough forest terrain and building ruins.

FEES: None.

PARKING/DIRECTIONS: The ruins are located along Broughton Road, by Loon Lake. After you turn right onto Broughton Road from Morrison Road, it's about a 6-minute drive along a gravel road. The easiest access to the town is at the point where Broughton Road veers left at a 90-degree angle to run parallel to Loon Lake (if you reach the private residence at 1179 Broughton Road, you've gone too far). You'll see a path into the forest on the right-hand side of the road, with yellow-sleeved guy wires at the left and several rocks to the right. There's no formal parking lot; park at the side of the road.

There are lots of paths and foundations to explore here. To see the Broughton Arms, walk past the first path to the right, and when you get to the next fork, take the right-hand path; a 2-minute walk will bring you to the expansive hotel ruins.

MORE: Sturdy shoes and tick checks are a must. As with any abandoned site, don't visit alone and be aware of your surroundings, as there are plenty of hazards to trip over. As there is little to no cell service, download maps in advance.

Broughton Arms Hotel, 1916.

44 Cape Breton Miners Museum:
Experience Life as a Coal Miner

WHAT

A museum that brings Cape Breton's mining industry to life through exhibits, an underground mine tour led by retired coal miners, a virtual simulator, and a replica of a historical mining village.

WHERE

17 Museum Street, Glace Bay, Cape Breton.

DETAILS

The first coal mine in Cape Breton opened over 300 years ago, and mining would play a key role in shaping the history of the island and

that of the entire province. Even today, in the aftermath of the mining industry, mining stories continue to be passed down from generation to generation, and the struggles of coal miners remain integral to the cultural identity of many Cape Bretoners. The Cape Breton Miners Museum pays tribute to this bittersweet legacy, bringing the coal mining industry and its poignant stories to life.

Above ground, a series of exhibits illustrate the history of mining in the area, featuring a collection of mining equipment. But the highlight of a visit to the Cape Breton Miners Museum is an underground tour of the on-site coal mine, which allows visitors to experience the dangerous conditions in which miners worked. A virtual simulator helps visitors learn more about life as a miner and even feel the effects of an underground disaster. All tours are run by retired coal miners, who share personal stories from their mining days and answer any questions posed by visitors.

Also on the property is the historic Miners' Village, where visitors glimpse miners' home life. A former company house has been restored

to illustrate the typical housing a miner and his family would have lived in at the peak of the mining industry. There's also a replica of a company store, a fixture in every mining community, infamous for exploiting underpaid miners by forcing them to buy all their essentials on site at inflated rates.

The Miner's Village Restaurant, located in a replica company house and decorated with period décor, including a rustic fireplace in the room's centre, is open seasonally. There's also a gift shop.

ACCESSIBILITY: The main building is fully wheelchair accessible; however, the underground mine has an uneven gravel surface, with a slight slope. The company store has a ramp for accessible entry, but the company house does not. The restaurant has a slight rise at the door, but once inside, it is accessible.
FEES: Admission is charged; the museum is open from June to October. For the remainder of the year, admission is by appointment only; contact staff in advance about a tour.

Main Floor Exhibits: Adult: $10 / Youth: $7. Virtual Mine Tour: Adults $20 / Youth: $15 / Family (of 4): $60. Underground Mine Tour (including Virtual Mine Tour): Adults: $25 / Youth: $20 / Family (of 4): $80. Children 5 and under can experience all activities for free.

Tours last between 90 minutes and 1 hour and 45 minutes, and during peak season they're based on walk-ins, so there are no set times; if you arrive at the museum before 4 p.m., you're guaranteed a tour spot.
PARKING/DIRECTIONS: Free on-site parking.
MORE: The underground portion of the site is a walking tour that starts at a height of 5 feet 6 inches: anyone taller than that should be prepared for crouching. Although visitors wear a hard hat equipped with a light, the tour may not be appropriate for anyone with an aversion to darkness or closed spaces.

The Men of the Deeps, Cape Breton's world-famous choir of working and retired coal miners, perform here throughout the warmer months. Visit minersmuseum.com for more information.

Room & Pillar Mining
In "Room and Pillar" mining, coal is removed in a checkerboard pattern leaving square "pillars" of coal to support the rock strata, or "roof", above the coal seam. The area from which the coal has been removed is called the "room", and it must be supported with pit props or the roof could collapse.
When coal is mined, dangerous gases are released which must be removed through ventilation. Air from the surface is directed to the mine workings using trapdoors similar to the one you just came through.

45 The Cape Breton TARDIS

WHAT

A faithfully replicated TARDIS from the science fiction series *Doctor Who*, recreated along with characters from the "Whoniverse" on a hill in rural Cape Breton.

WHERE

2984 NS-395, Scotsville, Cape Breton.

DETAILS

As the TARDIS can visit at any moment and any location in the universe, it's quite a compliment for the province that it chooses to remain in Nova Scotia.

The iconic time machine and spaceship, bearing the classic exterior of an antiquated British police box, is recognizable to fans of the science fiction series *Doctor Who*. And it's been recreated on a hill in rural Cape Breton—along with a few famous friends.

The TARDIS—or "Time and Relative Dimension in Space"—is the work of resident Colin Ogden, who was introduced to the *Doctor Who* universe (or "Whoniverse") by his wife, Viki, originally from England. Using materials he had lying around, Colin created the structure in 2015. Next came elaborate painted wooden cutouts of legendary *Doctor Who* villains: a life-size Dalek, Cyberman, and Weeping Angel, along with the faithful robot canine K9. There's even a huge reproduction of Van Gogh's *The Starry Night*, complete with a TARDIS appearance, as an ode to a specific *Doctor Who* episode.

The Cape Breton TARDIS has entertained visitors from around the

POLICE PUBLIC CALL BOX
POLICE TELEPHONE
FREE
FOR USE OF
PUBLIC
ADVICE & ASSISTANCE
OBTAINABLE IMMEDIATELY
OFFICER & CARS
RESPOND TO ALL CALLS
PULL TO OPEN

world. The couple has a Facebook page dedicated to it through which they share photos and updates. You can even enter the TARDIS—in fact, there's a guest book inside, along with a donation box—and see for yourself if it's actually bigger on the inside.

In 2025, the decade-old TARDIS was decimated by a storm. But, using stronger materials, including concrete and pressure-treated lumber, Colin rebuilt a newer, better version. TARDIS 2.0 includes an updated interior, including a mural and an interactive console.

ACCESSIBILITY: There aren't any stairs to access the TARDIS and friends, but the site sits on a grassy area that may be uneven.

FEES: None, although donations are gratefully accepted. This roadside attraction can be visited anytime; however, some of the *Doctor Who* villains may travel to warmer climes during the winter, so while you can still visit the TARDIS itself in the snow, for the full experience visit in spring, summer, or fall.

PARKING/DIRECTIONS: Free parking is available next door at the church, or park on the road at the side of the site. Located just before the East Lake Ainslie Cemetery and Church as you're driving north on Highway 395, you can't miss the huge, bright blue box at the side of the road.

MORE: Occasionally, scavenger hunts and other events are held at the Cape Breton TARDIS, so serious Whovians may want to visit the location's social media pages for more information. Visit facebook.com/capebretontardis for more information.

46 Gampo Abbey: A Cliffside Buddhist Monastery

WHAT

A Buddhist monastery on a seaside cliff just off the Cabot Trail, welcoming day visitors and offering a variety of retreats for students of Buddhism.

WHERE

1533 Pleasant Bay Loop, Pleasant Bay, Cape Breton.

DETAILS

Perched high on a cliff overlooking the Gulf of St. Lawrence stands something you probably wouldn't expect to find on the coast of Cape Breton: a Buddhist monastery.

Gampo Abbey was founded in 1983 by Chögyam Trungpa Rinpoche, in the Shambhala tradition; its collective goal is the creation of an enlightened society. A training ground for those new to Buddhism, as well as a place for experienced practitioners to deepen their study, the monastery also offers temporary and full monastic ordination. But everyone is welcome to stop by for a look at the abbey's grounds, trails, and exteriors.

Various short- and long-term residencies, programs, and retreats are offered, ranging from a week to several years, with different eligibility requirements for each, such as meditation experience and/or connection with a spiritual teacher. But whether a guest of the monastery as a lay person for a few weeks to experience life here, or perhaps as part of an intensive three-year retreat open only to ordained monastics, all residents at Gampo Abbey abide by the precepts of Buddhism. They also adhere to the monastery's rigorous schedule, taking part in purification

ceremonies, daily meditation, practice, study, chores, and observance of silence at certain times of the day. Day visitors, while not expected to observe silence while walking around the grounds, should be aware that, before lunch, monks may not wish to engage in conversation.

Visitors are free to wander the beautiful grounds, hike the trails, check out the stupa (a Buddhist shrine in the shape of a dome) with its stunning gold leaf details, and greet monastics. Visitors should obey the signs that declare certain areas off limits (such as paths to the cabins where solitary retreatants stay) and remain respectful during a visit, as this is a religious site.

ACCESSIBILITY: Visitors don't have to climb any stairs to enjoy the Stupa of Enlightenment or the paths on the abbey grounds. However, the ground may be uneven or muddy depending on the season.

FEES: None; can be visited year-round.

PARKING/DIRECTIONS: As with many hidden gems in Nova Scotia, your GPS may not be reliable in trying to direct you to Gampo Abbey. Drive to Pleasant Bay along Cabot Trail Road (NS-30). At the main—and only—intersection in Pleasant Bay is a sign for the monastery. Turn left onto Pleasant Bay Road, which eventually turns into Red River Road. About 9 kilometres later are the grounds of Gampo Abbey. There's free on-site parking and at the stupa.

To reach the Stupa of Enlightenment, either walk for 5 minutes down the road (slightly uphill) from the abbey parking area or simply continue driving down the road for a minute or two past the main entrance, until you arrive at the stupa, where there's parking adjacent to the plaza.

MORE: There is little to no cell service in the vicinity of the monastery and along much of the Cabot Trail, so plan your route before you go.

Before the COVID-19 pandemic, Gampo Abbey had been known to operate tours of the buildings and grounds, when the monastery's schedule permitted, but as of 2026, buildings remain closed to visitors. Visit gampoabbey.org for more information.

47 Giant MacAskill Museum: A Celebration of Cape Breton's Legendary Giant

WHAT

A museum dedicated to the 7-foot, 9-inch-tall Cape Breton giant Angus MacAskill, built on the site of his Cape Breton home and run by his descendants.

WHERE

504 NS-312, Englishtown, Cape Breton.

DETAILS

Cape Breton was once the home of the world's tallest giant, renowned not only for his height but also his incredible strength. You can visit Giant MacAskill Museum, built on the site of his home on Saint Anne's Bay, to learn all about him. There's a similar museum on the Isle of Skye dedicated to him, also run by his descendants.

Angus MacAskill was born in Scotland in 1825. As a young child, he immigrated to Englishtown, Cape Breton, with his family. Both of Angus's parents were of average height, and his own growth was nothing out of the ordinary until he reached his teen years, when he grew at a remarkable rate.

By the time he reached his early 20s, Angus stood 7 feet 9 inches tall and, throughout his adult life, weighed up to 510 pounds. His clothing and furniture, some of which can be seen in the museum, had to be specially made, and a removable transom was added to his home's front door to accommodate his height. There was no sign of characteristics of gigantism due to pituitary gland disorders, meaning that his height was proportional and "natural," not the result of a growth

GIANT
MacASKILL
"CAPE BRETON GIANT"
ANGUS MacASKILL
BORN IN SCOTLAND 1825
DIED AT ST. ANN'S CAPE BRETON 1863
HEIGHT---7FT 9IN.
BOOT---14½ IN.
GIRTH---80IN.
WEIGHT---425 LBS.

disorder; Angus is known colloquially as the tallest "true giant" to have ever lived. He even appears in the 1981 edition of the *Guinness Book of World Records*.

Angus, who possessed a gentle disposition, was a role model within the community. He reportedly embraced his legendary stature, choosing to work in show business as a featured performer with P.T. Barnum's Circus, and travelled around North America and Europe, even giving a demonstration to Queen Victoria at Windsor Castle. The Cape Breton Giant was famous for his displays of strength, one of which was lifting a 1,270-kilogram anchor, now on display in the museum. Eventually he moved back to Englishtown, where he bought a general store, grist mill, and other properties.

During a trip to Halifax in 1863, Angus suddenly became ill with what was diagnosed as "brain fever," likely meningitis or encephalitis in modern medical terms. He was brought back home to his parents' house, where his childhood bed was lengthened for him. He died in his sleep a week later. Angus was mourned not only by Nova Scotians but by the whole country, where he'd left a lasting impression on everyone he'd ever met.

Giant MacAskill remains a beloved icon for all Cape Bretoners. The Giant MacAskill Museum stands on a portion of Angus's original property in Englishtown. Visitors can see clothing and furniture that Angus used during his life, including his enormous bed frame and chair, and enjoy black-and-white photos of the legendary man, his family, and his home and other properties. There's a life-size handprint that you can compare with your own if you want to "high-five with the Giant" and a life-size statue of Angus. You may even luck out with a guide who is one of Angus's descendants—judging by the enormous family tree scrawled on the back wall of the museum, there are plenty of them—who can regale you with stories about Angus and his life.

ACCESSIBILITY: The building offers basic accessibility with a barrier-free entrance ramp.

FEES: Admission charged; open seasonally from May to September (by appointment only in May and June). If you're visiting at other months, contact the museum to see if they can accommodate you with an appointment.

Adult: $4 / Senior: $2.50 / Child: $2.50

PARKING/DIRECTIONS: Free on-site parking.

MORE: You can visit this gentle giant's final resting place in the Auld Cemetery in Englishtown, where a renovated site marker has replaced the original damaged gravestone, which can be seen in the museum.

Note: At the time of writing, the museum had temporarily closed for renovations but is expected to reopen for the 2026 season.

Visit giantmacaskillmuseum.com for more information.

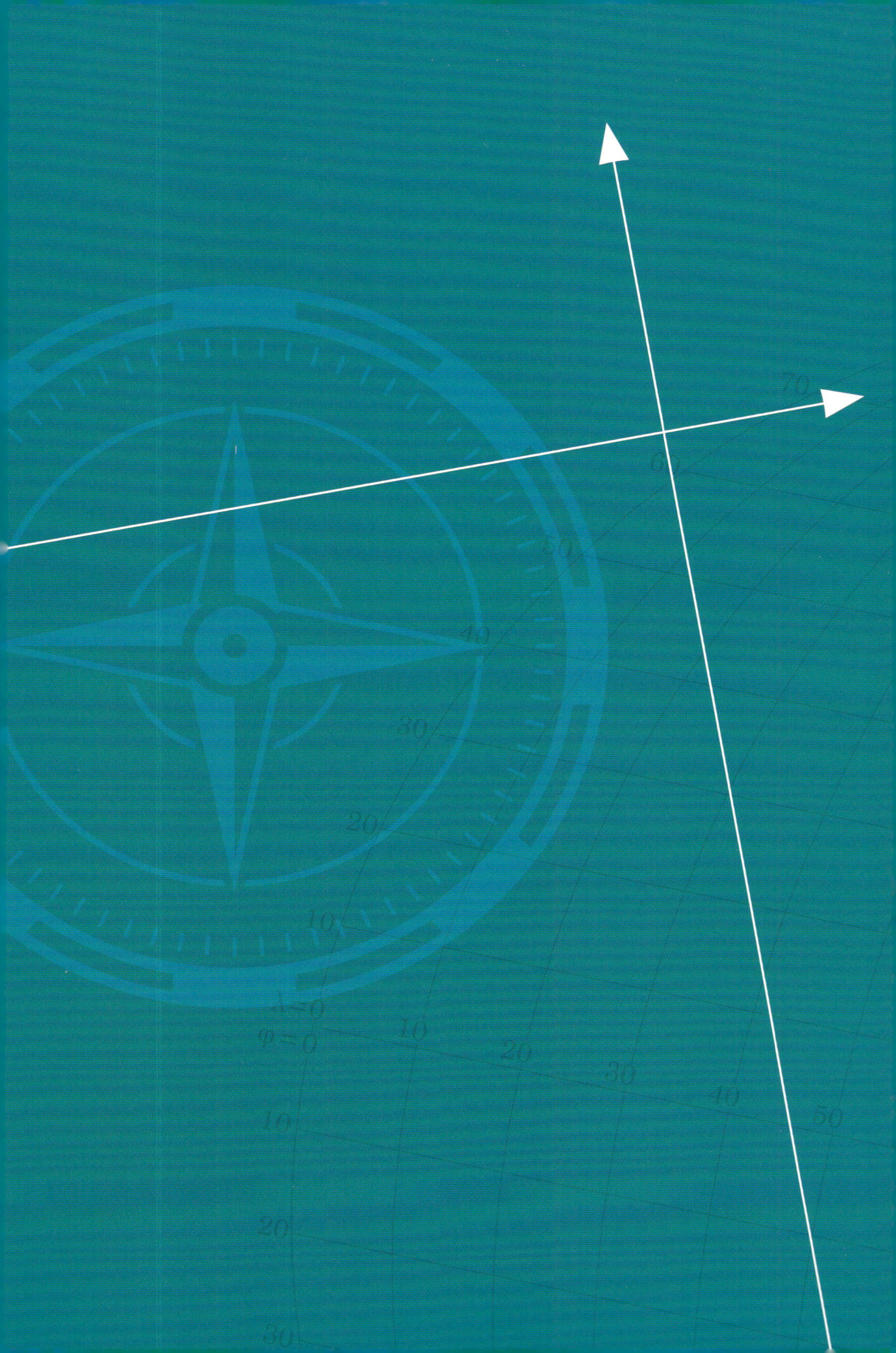

70
60
50
40
30
20
10
λ=0
φ=0
10
20
30
40
50
10
20
30

EASTERN SHORE

Stretching from Halifax to Cape Breton, Nova Scotia's Eastern Shore is an invigorating mix of untouched nature, hands-on history sites, and a picturesque coastline—with just a fraction of the residents and visitors in other regions of the province. Here you'll find the province's longest beach, the perfect waves for surfing, and a handful of unexpected and undiscovered gems.

48 Barry Colpitts's Folk Art House

WHAT

Award-winning folk artist Barry Colpitts's unmistakable house, covered in his colourful artwork.

WHERE

15359 Highway Nova Scotia Trunk 7 (Highway 7), East Ship Harbour.

DETAILS

It's impossible to miss artist Barry Colpitts's home if you're driving along Highway 7 on the Eastern Shore. The simple, white clapboard house is the backdrop for a joyous riot of brightly coloured folk art. Whimsical paintings and wood carvings of birds, fish, mermaids, fishermen, and boats cavort across every surface of the home (the porch, mailbox, and front yard aren't spared either), and there's a decided religious theme running through his work.

Colpitts started carving in 1989. Each piece has a story, and many represent family and friends. There are carvings of his wife and son, one of his uncle Bob, and even one of his mother, depicted while she was pregnant with Colpitts himself. But perhaps his most popular creations are his whirligigs, vibrantly coloured wind-powered delights (you can also set them spinning with a touch), guaranteed to bring a smile to every face.

Colpitts and his artwork have received many accolades over the years. His artwork has been featured in multiple publications, and he was awarded the King Charles III Coronation Medal in 2025.

The Nova Scotia Folk Art Festival used his art on their poster in

2009. Two of his whirligigs appear in the Beaverbrook Art Gallery in Fredericton, New Brunswick. The TV show "Weird Homes" filmed an episode on Colpitts's home in 2001, and his art appears in the 2009 movie *Nova Scotia Whirligigs*. One of his pieces (the "Eyeball Chair") is part of the Nova Scotia Art Gallery's permanent collection.

If Colpitts is home when you visit, he'll show you the outbuildings where he makes and stores his creations. He's happy to talk about his art and the inspiration behind them. In the summer, Colpitts sets up

a whirligig pasture in his yard, the perfect complement to his quirky home. He sells his artwork at festivals and galleries across Nova Scotia (including the Black Sheep Gallery in West Jeddore), but frequently sells out, so if you find his work for sale, pounce.

ACCESSIBILITY: This is a private residence, with a gravel driveway. The outbuildings are behind the house, up a grassy hill.

FEES: None, unless you're lucky enough to find a piece of Colpitts's art for sale.

PARKING/DIRECTIONS: Colpitts's house is located in East Ship Harbour, along Highway 7 (officially Nova Scotia Trunk 7). Coming from Halifax or Dartmouth, it's about 5 kilometres past the sign welcoming you to East Ship Harbour, on the left side of the road. As this is a private residence, there's no official parking lot, but you can park on the side of the road.

MORE: The *Open* sign on the lawn means that this famed folk artist is at home.

6

49 Memory Lane: A Snapshot of 1940s Nova Scotia

WHAT

A living history museum that brings 1940s Nova Scotia to life, depicting various facets of life on the Eastern Shore during and after World War II.

WHERE

5435 Clam Harbour Road, Lake Charlotte, just east of Musquodoboit Harbour.

DETAILS

Even if you can't remember the 1940s, you'll be charmed by the nostalgia of Memory Lane Heritage Village.

Owned and operated by the Lake Charlotte Area Heritage Society, this living history museum represents life in Nova Scotia during and after World War II. It's set up like a village, with paths connecting each location. There are 18 buildings to explore, each providing a fascinating glimpse into life in the 1940s. Although most of the structures date from before 1950 (some were saved from demolition to begin their new lives at Memory Lane), a few are replicas. Practice the three Rs in the one-room schoolhouse, enjoy a moment of contemplation in a time-worn pew in Clam Harbour United Church, make friends with the sheep, chickens, and kittens in the family barn, and marvel at the "latest amenities" in Webber House.

Use the village's Wi-Fi to access information about each location, including the history of the structures, how and from where they were moved to Memory Lane, and details about the faithful restoration work. Motion-activated soundscapes add to the immersive experience. Learn

about the industries that drove life on the Eastern Shore by visiting the prospector's cabin, boat shop (containing the in-progress replica of a 1940s' fishing boat), fisherman's storehouse complete with lobster traps and eel pots, and clam factory. You might even see—and smell—a fresh catch of fish curing in the sun.

Pose for a photo in the 1928 Ford Model A, or by the iconic vintage gas pumps at the village garage. When you're hungry, the Cookhouse serves up delicious and hearty meals in a rustic venue featuring reproductions of World War II propaganda posters. The Hosking General Store offers a variety of take-home memorabilia, much of it nostalgia-inducing, like the 1940s-themed games and candy.

Memory Lane hosts special events throughout the year, including clam-digging adventures, Heritage Spotlight Series, Supper and Spotlight Series, and Eastern Shore Players productions. Freshly made sugared donuts are often offered free of charge during special events. Whenever you visit, you'll enjoy the extensive knowledge of the costumed guides, who are happy to answer questions and lead you through demonstrations of era-appropriate activities (such as panning for gold and washing clothes in a wringer washer).

ACCESSIBILITY: The site is wheelchair accessible, with the exception of the second floor of Webber House. You may encounter uneven ground on parts of the outdoor paths.

FEES: Admission is charged for regular visits; open from June to September, and for occasional events throughout the year (such as traditional 1940s Christmas dinners).

Adult: $12 / Senior (60+): $10 / Youth (6–17): $5 / Child (0–5): free / Family (2 Adults, up to 3 Children): $30 / Groups (10 or more by reservation, with 24-hour advance notice): $9

There's free admission for select special events (Dominion Day, Walk through Christmas Past). Other events, including arts festivals, theatre and music events, and heritage talks with Cookhouse suppers, have separate pricing.

PARKING/DIRECTIONS: Free on-site parking.

MORE: The Eastern Shore Archives are on site and available by appointment for those conducting historical or genealogical research on the area.

Various locations in the village can be rented out for events. Visit visitmemorylane.ca for more information.

50 Nova Scotia's Secret Paradise: The 100 Wild Islands

WHAT

A little-known archipelago of nearly 300 pristine islands off Nova Scotia's coast, largely unchanged for the last 10,000 years.

WHERE

Between Clam Harbour and Mushaboom Harbour/Taylor Head Provincial Park on the Eastern Shore.

DETAILS

Hundreds of islands, virtually untouched since the last glaciers retreated, many with stunning white sand and crystal-clear water, hiding in plain sight off Nova Scotia's Eastern Shore? It sounds like fiction, but it's fact. And it's one of the province's best-kept secrets.

Few visitors and residents who aren't local to the Eastern Shore have heard of the 100 Wild Islands. The name is a misnomer, since there are actually nearly 300 islands in this extensive archipelago. Sprinkled across a 30-kilometre stretch of coastline with an total area of over 45,000 acres, the islands are noteworthy for being one of the few island groups left on the continent with such ecological richness, size, and undisturbed condition. And this is not a case where most of the islands are little more than glorified rocks that disappear at high tide. In fact, many of the islands are over an acre—some over 500 acres—in area.

The 100 Wild Islands boast a dizzying array of ecosystems and landscapes. Coastal barrens, bogs with carnivorous plants, glacial erratics, coastal rainforests, white sandy beaches, salt marshes, cold-water coral, and eelgrass beds are all found here. More than 120 species of birds call these islands home; some islands have their own freshwater lakes.

There's a balance to be struck between sharing these hidden island gems with the public and ensuring that tourists don't destroy them. Some of the islands are owned by the Crown and protected through their inclusion in the Eastern Shore Islands Wilderness Area. Others, once in private hands, have since been acquired and protected through

Nova Scotia Nature Trust's 100 Wild Islands Legacy Campaign, which complements efforts by the provincial government. In total, nearly 90 per cent of the islands in the archipelago are now permanently protected.

Access to the 100 Wild Islands is by water only. Kayaking and boating are popular ways to explore the islands, and visitors often use Tangier (specifically, the government wharf, although that has recently fallen into disrepair and caution should be exercised) and Murphy's Cove as launch points. Local outfitters such as Coastal Adventures offer sea-kayaking tours and expeditions, and Murphy's Camping on the Ocean offers several different boat-tour options for visitors wanting a short island excursion or a camping adventure.

A few islands in the archipelago are privately owned, although these are typically smaller, forested islands that wouldn't be suitable for camping or disembarking. Consult a map of the area (available from Nova Scotia Nature Trust or Eastern Shore Islands Wilderness Area, or from your outfitter) and stick to protected islands on your explorations. Fortunately, these include some of the largest and most picturesque: Tangier Island, Middle Island, Gooseberry Island, Wolfe's Island, Baltee Island, and Borgles Island.

ACCESSIBILITY: The islands are all undeveloped and the only trails are footpaths and old logging trails, which aren't suitable for wheelchairs. There is no infrastructure on any of the islands, and access can be gained only via boat.

FEES: None to access the islands, although any boat tours with local companies will involve costs; visit murphyscamping.ca/ocean-experiences, coastaladventures.com, and similar local organizations for options and pricing.

PARKING/DIRECTIONS: Vary depending on your launch location.

MORE: Visitors should give a wide berth to nesting colonies of seabirds. Be aware that there may be rocks and other submerged hazards that you might not see, if you're approaching by watercraft. Visit 100wildislands.ca for more information.

51 Spry Bay's Ancient Miniature Sand Volcanoes

WHAT

Hundreds of ancient tiny sand volcanoes, fossilized on a rock face along a coastal hiking trail.

WHERE

Spry Bay Trail, part of Taylor Head Provincial Park, 1000 Taylor Park Road, Tangier (southwest of Sheet Harbour).

DETAILS

They may not look like much, but the tiny, fossilized sand volcanoes along Spry Bay Trail are a fascinating, rare geological formation that was millions of years in the making.

Five hundred million years ago—millions of years before the first dinosaurs roamed the earth—hundreds of tiny underwater eruptions occurred on the ocean floor in what is now Taylor Head Provincial Park. These small sand volcanoes, or sand boils, were preserved in rock, and this is one of the only places in Nova Scotia where you can see this uncommon geological feature.

Spry Bay Trail's sand volcanoes were formed during a geologically turbulent time, when a supercontinent (in the middle of which was located the area we now call Nova Scotia) was in the process of breaking apart, creating new oceans as rifts formed. During this process, underwater avalanches caused currents to carry sand, silt, and clay sediments into deep water, where the currents weakened and the sediments settled. This process was repeated, and more sediments were dropped, until the layers were several kilometres thick. This

exerted enormous pressure, squeezing water out of the lower layers and forcing it upward, where it erupted, creating a landscape of sand volcanoes on the ocean floor.

One hundred million years later (still long before the dinosaurs appeared), landmasses collided again, and the sand volcanoes were folded into the Acadian Mountains, which may have been as tall as today's Alps. Over time, these mountains eroded, although you can still see vestiges of them (for example, in the province's Cobequid Mountains and the Cape Breton Highlands). Today, what was once a flat ocean floor and then a towering mountain is now an inclined rock face littered with the fossilized remains of countless sand volcanoes. Look for small bumps on the rock face, repeated over and over again—those are the sand volcanoes.

The sand volcanoes at Taylor Head Provincial Park are located close to the end of the Spry Bay Trail loop, near where it returns to the parking area. For a short hike, take the last part of the trail (heading counter-clockwise on the loop, if you're looking at a map), which will take about 40 to 50 minutes round-trip. For a more challenging hike, tackle the entire Spry Bay loop, which is about 4 kilometres long and will take between 90 minutes and 2 hours.

ACCESSIBILITY: Spry Bay Trail, including the section leading to the sand volcanoes, is not wheelchair accessible. The ground is uneven and can be muddy, and the forest trails are full of exposed roots and rocks. Viewing the sand volcanoes requires walking out onto uneven rocks along the shore, where it's easy to lose your footing.

Taylor Head Beach is also not wheelchair accessible, although there is a wooden boardwalk leading to the sand.

FEES: None; the main gate to Taylor Head Provincial Park is open seasonally from May to October, but the trail and park remain open year-round. Off-season visitors can access the park via Old Taylors Head Road.

PARKING/DIRECTIONS: Free on-site parking. You may see the address listed on your navigational device as 20140 Highway 7, Spry Bay; be aware that this takes you only to the start of Taylor Park Road, and you'll need to drive another 10 minutes to the parking lots.

Park at the last parking lot (lot #4) and take the boardwalk toward the beach. Once you pass the changerooms on your right, you'll see a path and map/signage on your right. This is the trailhead. After a few minutes (you'll pass a small graveyard from the early 1800s on your left), you'll see another map/signage on the trail; take the path into the forest on the right. In about 10 or 15 minutes, you'll arrive on a ledge overlooking the ocean, with a bench. To your left, you'll see a staircase and rock face to its right—continue walking for several more minutes, either along the forest path or along the rocks, until you arrive at the bottom of the stairs and the sand volcanoes scattered across the rock wall beside it.

MORE: Be sure to wear sturdy shoes and be aware that the path can be muddy depending on the weather.

The trails in Taylor Head Provincial Park cover a variety of landscapes: marshes, coastal barrens, forests, and beaches. Taylor Head Beach, reached by the same boardwalk you use to get to Spry Bay Trail, is one of the most stunning white sand beaches in the province and worth seeing while you're here.

reach for stars
MALM
To the Castle

Acknowledgements

A book like this can't be written without behind-the-scenes assistance of numerous excellent humans. I'm deeply grateful for their contributions, especially:

Jason, my sounding board, my travel companion, my chef when I lost track of meal times, my cheerleader, my technological guru ... my everything.

My brother Trevor, a valuable second set of eyes and the perfect guinea pig during his every visit to Nova Scotia.

The amazing team at Boulder Books, especially my fabulous editor, Stephanie Porter, for her tireless attention to detail.

My dear friend Greg Bellefontaine, who (literally) dreamt about me writing this book years ago, and supported me every step of the way as I made it a reality.

Mom, for her unwavering faith in me and this book, even (especially) when I didn't share it.

Abby Langille, for the perfect historical photo of Thinkers Lodge.

Troy McNutt, for his generosity and the fabulous drone footage.

Lucy Burgess, for hunting down wonderful vintage photos of hockey teams at Stannus Street Rink.

Dad, for his enthusiastic book ideas and for instilling in me a lifelong sense of joy and wonder about the world. He would have been thrilled to see this book completed.

All the people who work to keep the sites featured here up and running, often with little funding and while navigating global pandemics and unsettling economical and political times. Your efforts are appreciated more than you know.

And finally, to you, the reader, for choosing the road less travelled. May you always reap the rewards, and never stop exploring.

About the Author

Stacy Ann Milford is a Nova Scotia-based fiction and non-fiction writer whose work reflects the magic and mystery of the Atlantic landscapes around her. A passionate explorer, she has travelled, worked, and lived all over the world. Along the way, she has discovered that some of the best adventures can be found right in her own backyard, where she delights in uncovering Nova Scotia's lesser-known sites and their fascinating tales. Stacy has degrees in music, anthropology, and social work, and her short fiction has appeared in *Flash Fiction Magazine* and the anthology *Strangers in the Fog*. Visit stacyannwrites.com for more information.